A Concise History of
The Russian Orthodox Church

Neil Kent

*Do Michael
on your birthday
from Neil*

11. 3. 2024.

A Concise History of
The Russian Orthodox Church

Neil Kent

Academica Press
Washington ~ London

Library of Congress Cataloging-in-Publication Data

Names: Kent, Neil (author)
Title: A concise history of the russian orthodox church | Neil Kent
Description: Washington : Academica Press, 2022. | Includes references.
Identifiers: LCCN 2020056523 | ISBN 9781680539059 (hardcover) |
9781680539066 (paperback) | 9781680539073 (e-book)

Contents

Illustrations – A Concise History of The Russian Orthodox Church

The Baptism of Saint Prince Vladimir, Viktor Vasnetsov (1890)

Cathedral of the Dormition in the Monastery of the Caves, Kiev

Saint Sergei of Radonezh by Sergei Kirillov (1993)

Transfiguration, icon by Theophanes the Greek (15th century)

Virgin of Vladimir, icon by Andrei Rublev (1400)

Christ the Redeemer by Andrei Rublev

Christ's Harrowing of Hell by Dionisii (c. 1495-96)

Saint Philip II, Metropolitan of Moscow, icon

Solovetsky Monastery

Patriarch Philaret

New Jerusalem Monastery

Alexander Nevsky Monastery, St. Petersburg

Palace of the Most Holy Synod, St. Petersburg

Saint Tikhon of Zadonsk

Saint Philaret of Moscow.

Saint Nicholas of Japan

Saint John of Kronstadt

Davidov Pustyn Monastery of the Ascension, Novyy Byt

Metropolitan Tikhon of Moscow

Metropolitan Anthony of Sourozh

Foreword

Metropolitan Hilarion of Volokolamsk

A Concise History of the Russian Church, by University of Cambridge Professor Neil Kent, is a short account of the history of the Russian Orthodox Church, beginning with its origins in the tenth century and culminating in the modern period of the Moscow Patriarchate. The Church includes millions of faithful not only in Russia, but also in Ukraine, Belarus, Moldova, the Baltic countries, Central Asia, and everywhere else Russian Orthodox Christians have settled following the disasters of the twentieth century.

Throughout the Church's thousand-year history, it has endured many trials while inviolably preserving her unity. At times of internecine warfare among the Kievan grand princes, and during two centuries of Mongol rule, it was the Church that served as a source of support and comfort for the peoples of Holy Russia.

For centuries, the Church of Russia came under the jurisdiction of the Patriarchate of Constantinople, but in 1448 it faced the necessity of having to acquire its own primate. This came about as a result of the Council of Florence and the union of the Church of Constantinople with the Roman Catholic Church. The autocephalous status of the Russian Orthodox Church was later recognized by the Church of Constantinople, and in 1589 the Metropolitanate of Moscow was elevated to a separate Patriarchate by decision of the four traditional patriarchs of Eastern Christiandom.

Since then, the Moscow Patriarchate has united all the Russian lands, as recognized in a letter of 1654 from Patriarch Paisius of Constantinople to Patriarch Nikon of Moscow, in which the latter was designated "Patriarch of Moscow, and of Great and Little Russia." As new lands were joined to Russia, the Church's pastoral mission spread to new peoples, embracing within its spiritual scope the native inhabitants of Siberia, the Far North, the Far East, Central Asia, Alaska, Japan, Korea, and China.

Including the history and most important figures of the Russian Church in the period preceding the tragic events of the Revolution of 1917, Professor Kent describes Soviet persecution of the Orthodox faithful as the "path of the Russian Church toward Calvary."

Having endured some of the worst persecutions in Christian history, by the end of the twentieth century the Moscow Patriarchate enjoyed an ecclesiastical Renaissance, which has continued to the present day. The Calvary of long-suffering Russian Orthodoxy was followed by its Resurrection. This period of rebirth is described in detail in the book's concluding chapters.

While many works have been written on the history of the Russian Orthodox Church, the distinguishing feature of Professor Kent's book is its brevity and accessibility. It will be of great benefit for those who wish to familiarize themselves with our faith.

† Hilarion (Alfeyev), Metropolitan of Volokolamsk

Chapter 1

Introduction

All Christian Churches trace their origins to the life of Jesus Christ, and His Death and Resurrection, over two thousand years ago. For adherents of Christianity, these are the central events in the history and salvation of mankind.

Yet over the millennia, Christians have separated themselves from each other, not only by virtue of the political, cultural, and social diversities that distinguish them, but with differences of dogma, doctrine, and religious customs that developed over this long period. Already in the early centuries of the first millennium AD, the Church in the Eastern regions of the Roman Empire had developed characteristics that defines it to this today, in distinction to the Latin tradition that characterized the Empire's Western regions until the outbreak of the Protestant Reformation in the early sixteenth century. This latter, on-going event, which took centuries rather than decades to complete, destroyed the hegemony of the Roman Catholic Church in Western and Northern Europe and elsewhere in the Christian world. In its wake, Protestant religions, such as Lutheranism, Calvinism, Anglicanism, and the evangelical Baptist, Methodist, and other free church movements have strongly defined Christianity in the West. Yet in the modern world, they have all retreated before the onslaught of secularism, atheism, and agnosticism.

In the East, by contrast, Orthodoxy, has long since been the principal Christian faith, despite threats to its existence from Arab, Mongol, and Turkish conquests; attacks from Poland-Lithuania, Sweden, and Germany; and rule by militant atheistic communism. Now, in contrast to the atrophying practice of Christianity in the West, Orthodox Christianity in the East, especially in Russia, Belarus, Ukraine, Romania, Moldova, Bulgaria, Georgia, and parts of the former Yugoslavia, has experienced an extraordinary post-communist revival. The Russian

Orthodox Church under the Patriarch of Moscow, the subject of this book, has risen like a phoenix from the ashes to which it had been reduced by the Soviet regime in the wake of the Russian Revolution of 1917.

Establishment of Christianity in the Roman Empire

Throughout the first three centuries of Christianity, adherents of the faith suffered persecutions at the hands of Roman emperors and within the communities in which they lived. It was only in the early fourth century that their situation changed dramatically. In 312 AD, Emperor Constantine ceased persecuting Christianity and soon established it as the state religion of the Roman Empire, supplanting various forms of paganism that had characterized the empire and the republic before it.

Yet already by this time, factions were undermining the unity of the Church. In 325 AD, Constantine convoked an episcopal council of some 318 bishops, the heirs to the Apostles, who oversaw the rites and beliefs of the Church, as well as the priests who performed its sacraments. This was the Council of Nicea, then a Greek-speaking city in northwestern Anatolia, in what is today Turkey. The Nicene Creed, which emerged from the council, has ever since been the central expression of belief of virtually all Christians, namely its explication of the Trinity – the core belief for comprehending the mystery of the unity of God, in three persons, the Father, the Son, and the Holy Ghost.

Nicea was one of a number of early Church councils informing the dogmas, doctrines, and canons that still serve as the foundation blocks of all Christian churches to this day. Along with later ones, it also helped to define, often in open conflict, the relationship between Church and State.

According to the synoptic gospels of the Bible, Jesus had said: "Render unto Caesar the things that are Caesar's, and unto God the things that are God's."[1] In line with this, and as formulated by the Emperor Constantine, the relationship was perceived as one of harmony and complementarity. Constantine spoke of a "symphony" between the two, which, although it later occasionally broke down, would be reconfirmed in the ninth century, in the reign of Emperor Basil I (867-886 AD). In the reality of a world in which might frequently triumphs over right, however,

---

[1] Matthew 22:21

the relationship functioned most smoothly when the authority of the emperor, representing the state, was accepted and the patriarch, the first amongst the bishops of the church, submitted to his will. When this did not happen, great upheavals could result, both theological and political. This state of affairs was to characterize not only the ancient Church of Byzantium, but that of Russia a millennium later as well, especially under Tsars Ivan IV (1533-1584) and Peter I (1682-1725 – the "Terrible" and "the Great," respectively – and during the Soviet period in the twentieth century (1917-1991). In those dark times, torture, imprisonment, and death could await clerics unwilling to accept the heretical beliefs or un-Christian actions of state authorities who rebelled against Orthodox belief and morality.

The Cathedral of the Holy Wisdom or Hagia Sophia

From the fourth century AD until the conquest of the Byzantine Empire by the Turks, the Cathedral of the Holy Wisdom or Hagia Sophia, in Greek, was and in some respects, still is the greatest of all Orthodox Churches, the Mother Church of the Byzantine Empire. Moreover, it has for centuries been the symbol for the faithful dreaming about an Orthodox Revival in Constantinople, today's Istanbul, in what is now an overwhelmingly Muslim Turkey.

This most famous and venerable of all Orthodox churches was built by order of the Emperor Justinian I ("the Lawgiver") in 532-537. It is a vast and imposing stone edifice, with joints of brick and mortar, including elements of sand and ceramics. Its central feature is its nave, crowned by a vaulted central dome, in turn surrounded by smaller ancillary domes, richly decorated with icons. It served as the seat of eastern Christianity from the time of its completion until the fall of the Byzantine Empire to the Ottoman Turks in 1453. It was then turned into a mosque, with minarets added and its frescoed icons covered up. From 1935 to 2021, however, it was a museum, perhaps the most visited in Turkey, not only by secular tourists but by faithful adherents of Orthodoxy, especially those from Russia and Ukraine. All that, however, is set to change, since this mother of all Orthodox cathedrals has just been returned to use as a mosque by order of the Turkish government.

Early Church Fathers

Many threats to Orthodoxy over its long history were external to the Church but some came from within. Great spiritual leaders of the early Church did their best to safeguard the Eastern Church's teachings when confronted by the onslaughts of perceived heresy emanating from within the wider Christian community. Thus, Saint Basil the Great (330-379 AD) fortified the Church in its fight against the Arian heresy, which rejected a belief in the Trinity and saw Christ as subordinate to God the Father and created by Him in time. Another was the great theologian Saint Gregory of Nazianzus (c. 329-390 AD), Archbishop of Constantinople, who played a leading role in formulating the concept of the Trinity at the Council of Nicaea. Saint Gregory of Nyssa (c. 335-c. 394 AD) was also highly important for his theological contributions, not least for his theology of the Holy Trinity and his focus on the possibility of universal salvation. He was followed by Saint John Chrysostom (c. 347-407), another Archbishop of Constantinople, an ascetic figure who denounced vice wherever he saw it, even in imperial circles, and was the greatest preacher of his age.

Yet even when the emperor allowed the ecclesiastical councils to function without undue interference, serious issues could arise from other quarters within the Church. This happened, for example, when the resolutions of the Council of Ephesus, promulgated in 449, were rejected by the Assyrian and other eastern churches, as was that of the Council of Chalcedon in 451. The former confirmed the truth of the Nicene Creed and condemned the heresy of Nestor which perceived the divine and human natures of Christ to be distinct. The latter condemned the heresy of monophysitism, which maintained that Christ has only a divine nature.

Conflicts within the Early Church

One of the first "national" churches to split from the main corpus of the Christian communion was the Armenian Church. This happened due to the Council of Chalcedon which further maintained that Jesus is perfect in both his divinity and humanity, that is, as both God and Man. In contrast to both Latin and Byzantine church traditions, which accepted this, the

Armenian Church did not. This lead, in 506, to one of the early schisms (following that of Arius and the Donatists) which has rent Christianity to this day. A rift had already emerged, however, between Constantinople and Rome, seat of the Primate of Rome, Felix III. His rival, Patriarch Acacius (d. 489 AD) was deposed, resulting in an excommunication that severed the eastern capital from Rome, on an ecclesiastical level, from 484 AD to 514 AD and was never fully resolved. Paradoxically, it was Rome that safeguarded Orthodoxy, as we understand it today, while the patriarchs of Constantinople then often tended to fall into heresy.

While some Byzantine emperors were stalwart supporters of Orthodoxy, others were not. Emperor Constans II (641-668 AD) adopted the Monothelitic Heresy, which originated in Armenia and Syria. It purported that Christ had only one will, a doctrine condemned by Pope Martin I, along with the famous theologian Maximus the Confessor, in the Lateran Council of 649 AD, in which the emperor was given no role. The emperor's arm was long and, outraged by the pope's rejection of his stance, he had him forcibly removed to Constantinople, where he was tried in 655 AD. Escaping the death penalty, the pope was exiled to Chersonesus, in Crimea, the location where some two and a half centuries later Grand Prince Vladimir of Kiev was said to have adopted Byzantine Christianity as his faith and that of Rus. Later, in 658 AD, Maximus was also condemned and exiled to Colchis, on the Western coast of the Black Sea, in today's Georgia. Four patriarchs of the east supported the heresy: those of Constantinople, Alexandria, Antioch, and Jerusalem, while the Bishop of Rome maintained the traditional position.

In the following century, an even more disruptive heresy, Iconoclasm, emerged in 726 AD and hit full stride during the reign of the Emperor Constantine V (called "Copronymus," or the "dung-named" by those whom he persecuted, 741-775 AD). Inspired by the prohibition of graven images in both the Old Testament and Islam, the heresy utterly rejected the use of pictorial and sculptural images of God, the Blessed Virgin and saints in worship. Iconoclasts destroyed icons and other religious images which had aided the faithful in their spirituality for centuries. Iconoclasm had been promulgated by the Ecumenical Council of 754 AD, under Constantine V. In Rome, however, the pope rejected this heretical perception of icons, and the eastern Church revised its views on the subject after the death of the Emperor Theophilos in 842 AD.

While it lasted for nearly a century, Iconoclasm was finally defeated. The traditional beliefs, which in this case were supported by Rome rather than Constantinople, won out over those of the emperor and his supporters. As Saint John of Damascus had put it in the seventh century, "It is not for the King to lay down the laws of the Church ... it is the office of the King to provide a good civil order, but the ecclesiastical rules of the Church are a matter for the clergy and those in its magisterial positions."[2]

After Iconoclasm, the Church returned to its historic traditions with regard to icons and images and eventually achieved a consensus among Byzantine priests, monks, and laity based on the dogma, doctrines, and resolutions of ecumenical councils held over the previous four centuries. Nevertheless, another problem persisted: in a multiethnic empire, where multiple languages were used by various ethnic groups, linguistic confusion frequently played havoc with doctrinal proclamations, leading to misunderstandings and even violence, especially when aggravated by conflicts of politics, personality, and local customs.

Rise of Monasticism

From the time of the early ecumenical councils onwards, and throughout the first millennium of Christianity and beyond, monasticism assumed an important role in the Church. In the middle of the sixth century, there were 76 monasteries in Constantinople, with no fewer than 100,000 monastic faithful throughout the Byzantine Empire as a whole.[3] Their spirituality, dogma, and doctrine were based, as was true of the eastern Church, on two forms of apostolic succession, one based on that as promulgated by the bishops of the Church, from one generation to the next, and the other as conserved by the monastic fathers and mothers.[4] It was possible, during

[2] Giovanni Damasceno, *Secondo discourse*, in *Difesa delle imagine sacre*, pp. 103-105; 108-109, cited in Ilarion Alfeev, *La Chiesa Ortodossa* Vol. 1, p. 87.
[3] Alexander Dmitrievich Shmeman, *Istoricheskii put' Pravoslaviia* (Paris, 1987), pp. 144, 255.
[4] Kallistos T. Ware, "The Spiritual Father in Stain John Climacus and Saint Symeon the New Theologian," *Studia Patristica*, 18: 2 (1989), p. 299.

the Iconoclastic period, for the laity to unite with the monastic fathers to defeat heresy, for the monastic clergy preserved the Church's orthodox spirituality and beliefs far more faithfully than the emperors, patriarchs, and bishops. That said, the eastern monasteries remained subject to their bishops (as many do to this day), unlike those in the Latin West, which achieved administrative independence from local dioceses in favor of the religious order to which they belonged.

Soon another far more serious schism divided the Church. The rejection by the eastern Church of Rome's insertion of the *Filioque* into the creed, was its principal origin. According to this doctrine, the Holy Spirit proceeded both from the Father and the Son; in the eastern Church, the Holy Spirit proceeded from only the Father. In 863 AD, this theological conflict led to the deposition of Byzantine Patriarch Phótius I by Pope Nicholas I. This was unacceptable to the ecclesiastical authorities in Constantinople, who also rejected the *Filioque*'s insertion and a council was convoked to the pope in turn.

Politics also came into play. The pope died in 867 and that same year the Byzantine Emperor Michael III was assassinated and a new Emperor, Basil the Macedonian, himself forthwith deposed Phótius. A papally acceptable candidate who had previously held the position, Ignatius, was then placed upon the patriarch's throne. Two years later another council was convoked, this time with the participation of papal legates sent by the new pope Adrian II, temporarily healing the schism.

A crusade of proselytizing among the pagan tribes to the north took on renewed vigor at about this time. From the middle of the 860s, missionary activity was directed toward the Slavs and Bulgars, who had settled in what is today Moravia, in the Czech Republic, and throughout the wider Balkan region. Missionaries also made significant inroads in the territory which soon became known as the Principality of Rus, centered around Kiev.

Kiev's ruler Grand Prince Oleg was hostile to the Church, but a more favorable reception resulted in part from the establishment of a treaty between Rus and the Byzantine Empire, which encouraged trade. In the early tenth century, Kiev's first church was established, dedicated to the Prophet Elijah, a champion for the Hebrews against the Canaanites.

During a visit to Constantinople, Olga, the widow of Grand Prince Igor of Kiev and a ruler in her own right, became the first of the Rus princely house to adopt Christianity. She initially West for the procurement of missionaries to Rus. The German Bishop Adalbert arrived and, although his mission proved unsuccessful, other German missionaries followed, especially during the reign of Prince Yaropolk I.

With Rus becoming a significant military power to the north of Byzantium, it was not surprising that Emperor Basil II (976-1025) called upon Grand Prince Vladimir (r. 980-1015), when an internal revolt threatened to overthrow him. Vladimir pledged some seven thousand men on condition that he receive the emperor's sister Anna in marriage. Basil emperor agreed. The revolt was crushed, but with Basil reluctant to send his sister to Kiev, Vladimir used force to oblige Basil to comply. He did this by conquering Chersonesus, in Crimea, from the Byzantines. The consequences were immensely significant, in both religious and political terms. It was there that Vladimir was received into the Church in 988. Mass baptisms followed, and Vladimir was later canonized as a saint of the Church "equal to the Apostles," in commemoration of this event.

According to the famous *Chronicle of Nestor* – now thought by scholars to be a compilation from various authors writing in the late eleventh century – Vladimir, having found paganism wanting, sent emissaries to evaluate the principle faiths with which Rus had come in contact: Judaism, Islam, and Christianity, western and eastern. The first was rejected because the Jews had lost their sovereign territory. Islam's prohibition of alcoholic, along with other customs, went unpopularly against Russian customs. Christianity was the answer, but, according to the *Chronicle*, the eastern church's beautiful rituals surpassed those of Roman Church. Politics likely played a major role in the decision. Byzantium, one of the world's greatest empires, was also Rus's primary trading partner and controlled its only water communications with the outside world.

Whatever the circumstances of Vladimir's conversion, it proved an enduring feature of the Russian state. As Metropolitan Ilarion has written, "the choice of the 'Greek faith' would translate for the Russian people into a choice of civilization."[5] Vladimir's ambassadors at the Byzantine court had witnessed splendors ecclesiastical and imperial that the prince wished to adopt for Rus, and the Byzantine tradition has informed both the Russian Church and State down to our own day.

By no means all of this tradition had ancient roots. In the early days, for example, the congregation themselves sang liturgies. With the establishment of the Church as a state religion, however, choral singing was introduced, without the accompaniment of musical instruments. Prostrations, genuflections, and much of the ceremonial practices that accompany Orthodox rituals were adopted in Rus, for both religious and state occasions.

There was also the immensely important development of monasticism with roots in the early Church. As the eastern Church came increasingly under foreign threat, internally it experienced a period of great spiritual development, not least in the expansion of monastic life. It reached its greatest fruition in the monastic enclave of Mount Athos, in what is today northeastern Greece. Saint Athenasios the Athonite founded the renowned Grand Lavra Monastery there in 963, and many others were established in the following centuries, attracting monks from the four corners of the Orthodox world, including Rus.

---

[5] Metropolitan Ilarion, *Orthodoxy*, Vol. I (Moscow, 2016), 93.

Chapter 2

The Early Kievan Church

Establishment of the Metropolitan See of Kiev

Grand Prince Vladimir established the Metropolitan See of Kiev. Until 1589 it remained under the jurisdiction of the Patriarch of Constantinople. The first incumbent Metropolitan was Michael I (d. 992), who, tradition has it, was brought by Vladimir from Chersonesus. Of Bulgar or Assyrian ethnicity, he is said to have founded the city's first religious house, Saint Michael's Golden Domed Monastery. It is especially renowned for its glorious mosaic icon of Saint Demetrius, a Greek soldier martyred in the fourth century and commissioned in the eleventh century by Grand Prince Sviatapolk II, to commemorate his father Iziaslav I. The monastery's magnificent golden domes were among the first in Kievan Rus. The original cathedral, which was radically altered over the centuries, was destroyed on Stalin's orders in 1934 but was rebuilt after the fall of the Soviet Union and reconsecrated in 1999. In 2018, it became the seat of the Ukrainian Autocephalous Orthodox Church, which broke away from Moscow and placed itself under the authority of the Ecumenical Patriarch of Constantinople, a move that other Orthodox churches have declined to acknowledge as canonical.

Saints Boris and Gleb

Grand Prince Vladimir's death in 1015 opened the door to a vicious succession struggle. Kievan Rus did not practice primogeniture (Russia did not formally adopt it until 1797), but instead allowed for infighting over which candidate was the strongest and most capable. This system led to conflict among Vladimir's sons. Sviatopolk I assumed the throne after murdering his brothers Boris and Gleb, who, by refusing to resist, lived the principles of their faith. Canonized in 1071 as passion sufferers, they were the first saints of Rus.

Sviatopolk was in turn overthrown by another brother, Yaroslav, who reigned until 1054 and gave Rus its first law code and became known as "Yaroslav the Wise." Succession battles resumed after his death, but during the reign of his son, Iziaslav I, many Greek religious texts were systematically translated from the Greek, using the Cyrillic and Glagolitic alphabets as fostered by the Bulgar Saint Clement of Ohrid, but originally said to have been devised by the Macedonian monks Saints Cyril and Methodius in the ninth century. This linguistic adaptation helped to spread Orthodoxy throughout medieval Rus.

Monasticism also flourished in Rus. The Monastery of the Transfiguration, near Vyshhorod, was founded for Greek monks in 988, the same year of Rus's conversion. It later became one of the most important monasteries for the Cossack Zaporozhian Host and featured in some of Ukraine's most famous literary and artistic works, including Ivan Kozlov's poem "Chernets" and Nikolai Gogol's novel *Taras Bulba* (1835). It lasted in various forms until the Soviets demolished it in 1936.

Episcopal seats were also rapidly established at Novgorod and Polotsk, among other places. By the end of Vladimir's reign, some four hundred churches had been established in and around Kiev alone.[6]

Saint Hilarion

Saint Ilarion succeeded Theopemptus as Metropolitan of Kiev in 1049, with the support of Grand Prince Yaroslav the Wise. He was the first non-Greek appointed to the see, an uncanonical posting because it was made without the agreement of the Patriarch of Constantinople. Saint Luke Zhidiata (d. 1060), the second Bishop of Novgorod, refused to accept its validity, even though he himself was born in Rus, and in consequence was imprisoned at the Monastery of the Caves at Kiev until his death. Despite the irregularity of Ilarion's occupation of the metropolitan see, he has long been revered for his spiritual writings, *Sermons on Laws and Grace, Confession of Faith* and *Sermons on Spiritual Benefits to All Christians*. He was succeeded by Metropolitan Ephraim (1055-?).

---

[6] Ilarion, *Pravoslavie*, Vol. 1, 129.

The Cathedral of Saint Sophia in Kiev

Among the most important churches of Kievan Rus extant today is the Cathedral of Saint Sophia, built in 1037 and was completed some two decades later. Narrowly escaping demolition under the Soviets, it has been a museum since 1934, although, since the fall of the Soviet Union, church services are occasionally held there. Inspired by the Byzantine Cathedral of Saint Sophia in Constantinople, it unusually possesses five naves, each with its own apse, and the whole is crowned by thirteen cupolas, the number symbolizing Jesus and His Apostles. Eleventh-century mosaics and frescoes decorate its interior. They depict the family of Grand Prince Yaroslav, as well as figures kneeling in prayer. It also still preserves his remains, although the relics of other Kievan rulers are no longer there. It was devastated on various occasions in its history, by internecine struggles within Rus and in Polish-Russian conflicts. Nonetheless, it survived and in 1633 was given a Ukrainian Baroque exterior by the Italian architect Octaviano Mancini. Its Byzantine interior, however, was preserved. In the late eighteenth century, a bell tower was added.

The Great Schism

By the early eleventh century, Eastern Christianity was firmly established as the religion of Kievan Rus. Yet this occurred against a background of ecclesiastical fracture which has persisted into the present. In 1054, the Great Schism, which has split Orthodoxy from Roman Catholicism, with their seats based in Constantinople and Rome, respectively, finally consolidated a religious rending that has lasted for almost a millennium. On 5 July 1054, papal legates arrived at Constantinople's Cathedral of Saint Sophia and publicly excoriated the Patriarch Michael I Cerularius during the liturgy, excommunicating him for heresy, because of his refusal to incorporate the *filioque* in the creed. The Eastern clergy also felt conscience bound not to accept the Western doctrine of papal primacy. Conflicting traditions also aggravated the rift: the imposition from Rome of the celibacy of all clergy (official from 1215), the use of episcopal rings, and the rejection of beards. Refusing to accept Rome's judgment in these and other matters, the patriarch convoked a synodal council of twenty bishops who, in turn, excommunicated the papal legates and the Pope in Rome.

The schism was a dramatic ecclesiastical break, but in political terms the fracture between east and west had preceeded it by at least two centuries on a plethora of planes. In the east, the Byzantine emperors held sway, albeit confronted by Muslim encroachments; in the west, Charlemagne united much of the Western heartland of Europe, an accomplishment confirmed by Pope Leo III, who crowned him Emperor of the Romans in 800. Each half of Europe went its own way, spiritually, politically, culturally, and even linguistically – Latin and derivative Romance languages in the Holy Roman Empire and Greek in the shrinking Byzantine Empire in the east.

With the advent of the Crusades at the end of the eleventh century, an even darker period of conflict broke out between the estranged churches. Its culmination was the sack of Constantinople by the Roman Catholic armies of the Fourth Crusade, in 1204. A Latin patriarch was also imposed on the Byzantine capital at this time, which Western forces held for much of the century.

Kiev's Monastery of the Caves

Among the most significant of the early saints of the Russian Church was the ascetic Saint Anthony of the Caves (983-1073), under whose patronage the Church and Monastery of the Dormition of the Mother of God was established in the heart of a complex that is today the Kiev Monastery of the Caves. It was governed by the Abbot Theodore (1074), another ascetic cleric, venerated to this day, along with Saint Anthony, as a founder of Russian monastic life. Indeed, the Dormition was and remains one of the oldest and greatest cathedrals of Russian Orthodoxy, along with the Cathedrals of the Dormition in Vladimir and Moscow and Saint Sophia in Novgorod. As Rus's political capital, Kiev became the premier see and religious capital as well.

In Kiev, Church and State worked together. This symphony culminated in the middle decades of the twelfth century, especially under Prince Andrei Bogolyubsky (r. 1157-1174), a powerful figure who was eventually canonized for his defense of Christianity and its ecclesiastical hierarchy. By the early thirteenth century, some forty episcopal sees had been established in Rus, all ultimately answering to the Patriarch of Constantinople. After the Mongol conquest destroyed Kiev in 1240, religious authority shifted north, to Vladimir, which became the center of political power and religious authority, while Novgorod maintained some degree of political and religious autonomy.

Threats from West and East

Having adopted Christianity from Byzantium, Rus was also affected by the ecclesiastical upheavals to the south. In 1227, Pope Honorius III wrote to the Grand Prince of Kiev to secure permission for Catholic missionary activity at the eastern end of the Baltic Sea, in what is today Latvia and Estonia. This move sought not only to serve the Christian mission to convert the region's non-Slavic pagan tribes but also, they hoped, as a backdoor into Rus itself, enabling its integration into the Roman Catholic fold. German knights assembled in the Teutonic Order speedily conquered the region and established Catholic rule until the knights converted to Lutheranism in the sixteenth century.

A far greater threat to the faith of Rus, indeed, Christianity itself, was to make its epiphany in these decades, namely the Mongol invasions of Kievan Rus. Emerging from the Asian steppe, the Mongols defeated local tribes and their Rus allies in 1223 and returned to devastate the Rus realms 14 years later. After just three years of campaigning, the Mongols reduced the population to vassalage. The Mongols went on to devastate Poland and Hungary. Only a timely succession struggle prevented their ranks from conquering all of Europe.

Against this backdrop, in 1274 the Roman Catholic Second Ecumenical Council of Lyons sought, through a treaty with the Byzantine Emperor Michael VIII Palaeologus to end the schism. This attempt failed, and only rancor and discord remained, poisoning the relations of the two "lungs of Christendom" until our own day.

Chapter 3

The Russian Church
During and After the Tatars

The Mongol Conquest

The Mongol conquest of most of Rus – Novgorod and other northwestern territories alone escaping its ravages but not its political consequences – left a trail of untold destruction in its wake. Most major cities were devastated. Catastrophe struck Kiev on 6 December 1240, when Mongol hordes under Khan Batu, grandson of the Mongol warlord Genghis Khan seized the city. Metropolitan Kirill II (ca. mid-1240s-1281) fled. After his death, Metropolitan Maksim moved the see to Vladimir.

By this stage, however, the Mongols' military power aided the survival of Orthodoxy. When the Teutonic knights attacked Rus, occupying the city of Pskov, Mongol forces provided considerable military aid to the Prince of Novgorod, Saint Alexander Nevsky (c. 1221-1263). Battling the knights on Lake Peipus, which today forms the border between Russia and Estonia, Nevsky won an astounding victory and reversed their advance. Loyal to the Mongols, he became Grand Prince and delivered tribute to their capital at Sarai.

The Mongol subjection of most of Rus was exacting but also empowered a semi-autonomous Rus state. On the one hand, the Mongols obliged Rus to pay a heavy annual tribute to their Khan on pain of renewed attacks. By the early decades of the fourteenth century, the small principality of Moscow, established for Alexander Nevsky's youngest son Daniel, began a steady rise to dominance. Thanks to a series of highly competent leaders, it expanded its territory and cultivated the Mongols, who endowed it with political authority. When the Grand Prince of Moscow, Ivan I Kalita (r. 1325-1341) became the most powerful Russian ruler, Metropolitan Peter moved to Moscow from Vladimir, confirming Moscow as the most important city in Rus. It has remained Russia's holy capital ever since.

Saint Alexis the Wonderworker of All Russia

In spiritual terms it was Saint Alexis. (c. 1292-1378), Metropolitan of Moscow, known as a Wonderworker of All Russia, who was the most significant of early Russian prelates. Scion of the princely line of Chernigov, he joined the Theophany Monastery in Moscow, where the monks Gerontius and Saint Stephen became his spiritual guides. He eventually came to attention of Metropolitan Theognostus, who put him in charge of the ecclesiastical courts, which he administered for twelve years. In 1350, he became Bishop of Vladimir and in 1354, Metropolitan of Moscow. Like Alexander Nevsky, Saint Alexis also visited the Mongol court, where he was said to have miraculously cured the blindness of Taidulla, a consort of the khan. He also founded several monasteries, including that of the Icon of the Savior Not-Made-by-Hands, by the River Yauza, in Moscow, and the Chudov Monastery, in the Kremlin itself.

Saint Sergei of Radonezh

Another towering spiritual figure was Saint Sergei of Radonezh (c. 1314-1392). Descended from a noble family of Russian *boyars*, or lords, he exerted the greatest influence of any personage on the Russian Orthodox Church and its mission. In 1340, he founded what is today Russia's most venerated monastic house, the Trinity Monastery of Saint Sergei, at Sergeiev Posad, some seventy kilometers northeast of Moscow. Its ascetic rules were confirmed by Philotheius, the Ecumenical Patriarch of Constantinople. It is said that the benediction Saint Sergei bestowed upon Grand Prince Dimitrii (r. 1360-1389), and the aid of the monks Andrey Osliaba and Alexander Pesresvet, helped the prince to win the Battle of Kulikovo Field, near the River Don (for which he became known as "Donskoi") in what is now the province of Tula. This pivotal battle was fought against Khan Mamai in September 1380 and was a solid first step toward ending the Mongols' hegemony over Rus, which was by then indisputably identified with Moscow's rule. Mongol sovereignty was not yet lifted but tribute was reduced and Moscow had showed that it could successfully challenge its nominal overlords.

Theophanes the Greek

Theophanes the Greek (1340-1410) was the first of a triumvirate of extraordinary icon painters of Muscovy. Born in Constantinople, Theophanes first settled in Novgorod, in 1370, before moving on to Moscow in 1395. His icon *Christ's Harrowing of Hell* (1408) and the *Transfiguration* (1408) are amongst his most famous paintings and with their use of earthy colors have an extraordinary spiritually expressive quality.

Andrei Rublev

Theophanes's most renowned pupil was Andrei Rublev (1360s-1430). He helped enable, despite Moscow's continued subordination to the Mongols, a spirituality within the Russian Orthodox world through distinctive iconography. Rublev is considered one of the greatest icon painters of any period, and his images enable a spiritual depth and communion with God, His Mother, and the saints in the most extraordinary way and from which we, in equal measure, benefit in our own day. In 1405, he decorated the Cathedral of the Annunciation, in the Moscow Kremlin. Three years later, he travelled to Vladimir, where he worked at the Cathedral of the Assumption and produced masterpieces. His *Virgin of Vladimir* is his masterpiece of this period. Perhaps his greatest work, and one he executed without assistance, was his *Icon of the Holy Trinity* (c. 1410, now in Moscow's Tretyakov Gallery). Another great icon attributed to him is that of *Christ the Redeemer*, said to have been painted for a cathedral in Zvenigorod. Later Rublev worked at the Trinity Monastery's Cathedral of the Holy Trinity. His work fused Byzantine and Russian artistic traditions, influenced by his collaboration with Theophanes. He retired to the Andronikov Monastery, where he died in 1430. Over half a millennium later, in 1966, the great filmmaker Andrei Tarkovsky produced a Soviet cinematic masterpiece which, despite the atheism of the regime under which he worked, captures some of the great spirituality of this divinely gifted icon painter and his spiritually infused works that still speak to us today.

Dionisii

Dionisii (c. 1440-1502) was a third renowned icon painter. Among his earliest great works are icons at the Cathedral of the Dormition in the Moscow Kremlin. His most famous series of icon paintings was that done together with his sons at the Ferepontov Monastery, to the west of Vologda, particularly *Christ's Harrowing of Hell* (1495-96). His most important patron was Saint Joseph of Volokolamsk, who commissioned over eighty icons from him.

Failure of the Council of Florence to Reunite Christendom

Having weakened the Mongol yoke, Muscovy was alarmed by threats to Constantinople from the Ottoman Turks, who had adopted Sunni Islam. Over the previous centuries, more and more Byzantine territory had fallen to Islam, including most of its Balkan domains.

Against this background, in April 1438, an ecumenical council took place at Ferrara, in the Papal States, which sought to heal the Great Schism and reunite the churches. The Byzantine Emperor John VIII Palaeologus (r. 1425-1448) attended, presiding over representatives of the Orthodox Church. Among them, Metropolitan Isidore of Kiev (1385-1463), a native of the Greek Peloponnesus, was the most prominent. Agreeing on a common theology was the primary agenda, but discussions fell apart over the concept of purgatory.

In February 1439, after the council had been transferred to Medici Florence, the primary issue of the *filioque* was considered. According to this doctrine, the Holy Spirit issued from both the Father and the Son, a stance unacceptable to Orthodoxy. Bishop Mark of Ephesus (later canonized) remained adamant in his refusal to accept it. Nonetheless, debates and discussions continued into the summer and, with an offer of military aid by the Roman Catholic Western powers to the embattled Byzantines, the other 33 Greek ecclesiastics finally acquiesced, including Isidore and Patriarch Joseph of Constantinople.

Nevertheless, once the prelates returned home the restored unity was undone. Grand Prince Vasily II of Moscow (r. 1425-1462), joined by both the nobility and local churchmen, unequivocally rejected the reunion and declared Isidore's stance heretical. This repudiation was further bolstered in Constantinople, when a new church council held in 1450 formally overturned the union established by the Council of Florence and returned the Byzantine Church to Orthodox traditions.

Other Orthodox leaders shared in this condemnation of the Council of Florence, including the Patriarchs of Alexandria, Antioch, and Jerusalem. With hostility toward Catholicism now greater than even that arrayed against Muslims, it is no surprise that some, on the verge of the conquest of the Byzantine Empire, now looked to the Turks for support. The famous Byzantine statesman Loucas Notaras declared, "I prefer the reign of the Turkish turban to the Latin tiara." He might have spoken differently had he known that he would later be put to death at the order of the Sultan for the obduracy of his Christian convictions.[7]

Some resistance remained. Under threat of capital punishment by Tsar Vasily, under whom he was imprisoned for two years, Isidore fled to Rome, which then sent him to Constantinople as papal legate. He remained their until the Turks captured the city in 1453. Isidore returned to Rome, where he was made a Catholic cardinal and Bishop of Sabina, as well as titular Latin Patriarch of Constantinople and Archbishop of Cyprus.

After the Ottoman conquest of Constantinople, Moscow moved toward ecclesiastical independence, with metropolitans now installed in the capital without the approval of the Patriarch of Constantinople, setting the tone for Moscow's future claim to be the "Third Rome."

Meanwhile, a new metropolitan's see was established in Kiev, whose territory had been absorbed by the Polish-Lithuanian Commonwealth formed by a dynastic union in 1386. After the Council of Florence, Metropolitan Gregory became its first incumbent. In 1460, however, he was obliged by his flock to repudiate the Union, even though Rome had authorized usage of the eastern liturgy. The Kievan ecclesiastical leaders then subordinated themselves to the new Patriarch of Constantinople, who now reigned under Ottoman suzerainty and continued to retain formal authority over the Muscovite church as well. Kiev, however, did not rejoin Moscow and reasserted its ecclesiastical

[7] Ilarion Alfeev, *La Chiesa Ortodossa* (Bologna, 2013), p.146.

autonomy. The rift lasted until 1685, but its seams have reopened in our own times, stoked by local politics.

Politically, Moscow's isolation encouraged it to assume the mantle of the defunct Byzantine Empire and its spiritual leadership. This was particularly true from 1453, when the Sultan made the Patriarchate of Constantinople, Gennadios Scholarios, leader of the Greek *millet* (community) of the Ottoman Empire. This left Moscow the largest independent Orthodox state, a succeeding "Third Rome," at least as far as most of the Orthodox world was concerned. The marriage of Byzantine princess Sophia Palaeologus to Grand Prince Ivan III (r. 1462-1505) in 1472 symbolically strengthened this imperial claim.[8] Eight years later, in 1480, Ivan finally threw off the last vestiges of the "Mongol Yoke" after a victorious confrontation with the now deeply debilitated Golden Horde.

The Ukrainian-born monk Philotheus of Pskov (1465-1542), abbot of the Yelizarov Monastery and putative author of *The Legend of the White Cowl*, recounted this historic development. In his words, "The first Rome fell because of impiety, the second because of the assault of the descendants of Agar, the third Rome is Moscow and there will be no fourth."

---

[8] Ironically, it had been Pope Paul II who had encouraged this marriage, hoping that it would facilitate acceptance in Moscow of the Council of Florence.

Chapter 4

Conflict and Reform

Controversy over Monastic Wealth

In the early sixteenth century, a bitter theological controversy developed in Russia over the degree to which it was appropriate for monasteries to accumulate wealth, a practice that affected both church and state. Monastic life and the material resources of monasteries were at the center of this controversy.

Monasteries of this this period fell into one of two categories: the cenobitic, in which communities of monks live by a religious rule, and the hermetic, a reclusive, solitary, and ascetic form of monastic devotion. Poverty was, by Christian tradition, a virtue of the spiritual life for both variants, but how it was to be observed was often perceived differently. Monastic houses – and the wider Church itself – acquired land, money, villages, even slaves and, later, serfs through donations, bequests, purchases, and other forms of acquisition.

Perhaps the greatest hostility to ecclesiastical wealth came from the secular world, namely the rulers of Moscow and their acolytes. The Church's power rivaled that of the secular ruler, and its wealth sometimes allowed it to assert itself against the wishes of the Grand Prince. Ivan III wished to increase the Church's dependence upon the state, not only with respect to its finances but also in its political and religious aspects. The most important theologian to oppose this was Saint Joseph of Volokolamsk (1440-1515). He based his opposition not only on the need to resist the secular encroachment of the Russian *Caesar*, which was corrupted into the title of "Tsar," which came into informal use under Ivan III, but also to enable his monastery to continue its charitable activities, upon which so many people depended: Volokolamsk sustained some 700 people, including 50 orphans.[9]

The Judaizing Heresy

Another great Church controversy at the time was the "Judaizing Heresy." In this Saint Joseph of Volokolamsk offered a powerful defense of the Church in both its spiritual and temporal roles. Not only did he stand in opposition to this and other internal heresies, but he resisted Moscow's secular authorities when they became involved. Joseph perceived the Judaizing heresy as a great threat, for it was supported by some of the highest state officials in opposition to the authority of the Church. He was assisted by Saint Gennady of Novgorod (1410-1505), Archbishop of Novgorod and Pskov, who enjoyed great fame at the time for his Slavonic codex of the Holy Scriptures (the "Gennady Bible," 1499).

This heresy was said to be "Judiazing" in the sense that it rejected the doctrines of the Trinity and salvation through Christ's crucifixion and resurrection, among other tenets, while introducing into religious practice elements of traditional Jewish belief, worship, and practice, including circumcision. These practices and beliefs masked the reality of many hidden political and dynastic ambitions which lurked beneath the "religious" surface.

These false doctrines appear to have been first preached in Novgorod, a rich province that had maintained autonomy from both the Mongol invaders and Moscow after it became preeminent. The so-called *Secretum Secretorum* is also said to have played a major role. Purporting to be an Aristotelian treatise because it propagated many of the Greek philosopher's ideas to a wide European readership at that time, it was a recent pastiche.

Another important text was the *Aristotelian Gate.* Its translator is said to have been a Kiev-based Jewish scholar of that period, Judah al-Harizi, who used Arabic sources.[10] A Jewish visitor to Novgorod, one

---

[9] G. L. Fedotov, *I Santi dell'Antica Russia* (Milan, 2000), pp. 188-189.
[10] Russell Zguta, "The '*Aristotelevy vrata*' as a Reflection of Judaizer Political Ideology," *Jahrbücher für Geschichte Osteuropas*, 26: 1 (1978), pp. 2 and 4.

Scharija (Zechariah Ben Aharoohen), is said have also played a brief role in laying the groundwork for its propagation in 1470.

The arrival of troops from Moscow the following year had put a stop to the new ideas and, indeed, to Novgorod's independence. Nevertheless, the conversion of two local priests, Denis and Aleksei, proved fruitful for the heresy when, in 1483, Tsar Ivan III arrived and made their acquaintance. Through his entourage, they in turn, had become acquainted with Fedor Kuritsyn, Ivan III's secretary for foreign affairs, Elena of Moldavia, consort of his son Ivan the Young (d. 1490), and her son Dimitrii. Metropolitan Zosima of Moscow may also have taken an interest.[11]

Comparing the issue to perceived recidivism among the converted Moors and Jews of Spain at that time – a phenomenon that eventuated the greatest excesses of the Inquisition – some leading ecclesiastics resorted to draconian means to crush the Judaizers. Both Joseph and Gennady advocated the death penalty for apostates from Orthodoxy, specifically by burning at the stake, the favored ritualistic method of execution for heretics in Western Europe.[12]

The Jews as a people were not much affected by this policy for the simple reason that they were a rarity in Russia at this time.[13] Only after the the eighteenth-century partitions of Poland, under the Empress Catherine the Great, did Russia become home to most of Ashkenazic Jewry.

Saints Joseph of Volokolamsk and Gennady of Novgorod generally opposed Ivan III, not only for theological reasons but also because of his attempts to prevent the Church's acquisition of wealth. However, they were supported by him, a traditionalist, on the Judaizer question. A council was convoked in the presence of Ivan and his heir, who later reigned as Vasily III (r. 1505-1533), the son of Ivan's consort Sophia Palaeologus, daughter of the last Byzantine emperor. Various forms of heresy were condemned and made capital crimes, including the Judaizing heresy. Those who repented kept their lives but were imprisoned

---

[11] Ibid., p. 5.

[12] George Vernadsky, "The Heresy of the Judaizers and the Policies of Ivan III of Moscow," *Speculum* 8: 4 (1933), p. 441.

[13] *Iosif Volotskii, Prosvetitel, ili oblichenie eresi zhidovstvudzhushchich* (Kazan, 1903) pp. 533-539.

for penance. Prince Dimitrii, the son of Ivan's deceased older son, and his mother Elena of Moldavia were imprisoned (where both died), while notable officials who had adhered to the heresy were burned at the stake, along with Kassian, the Abbot of the Saint George Monastery.

Nevertheless, the heresy and the texts upon which it was based continued to circulate both in the Russian lands and abroad over the following decades. Aside from its religious and dynastic contexts, it also had another political one, which in the European *Zeitgeist* dovetailed well with monarchs seeking to introduce an Erastian view – later taken up by Peter the Great (r. 1682-1725) – which gave rulers ultimate control over the governance of both Church and State. This was certainly the case with Tsar Ivan IV "the Terrible" (r. 1533-1584). In any case, the heresy's political lessons, as well as similar ones in the *The Aristotelian Gate*, resonated with Russian monarchs who sought to crush the power of the churchmen, and with acolytes who resented their tyranny. In 1551, a church council was eventually convoked to deal with the heresy and the teachings of *The Aristotelian Gate* once and for all. They were unequivocally condemned as "satanic" in concept and "occult" in practice, but the political implications for the tsar's power remained and incumbents of the throne rarely hesitated to carry out their will.[14]

Saint Nil Sorsky

Not all Russian clergymen agreed with Saint Joseph of Volokolamsk and his policies. Saint Nil Sorskiy (1433-1508), one of the greatest theologians and spiritual leaders of his time, and still greatly admired today, objected to Joseph's severe approach to crushing heresy by subjecting heretics to death or imprisonment. He preferred the power of prayer and admonition to achieve their conversion. He also rejected the idea that the Church should acquire great wealth. Charitable donations were not to be conflated with spiritual life. Nil showed himself thereby to be a true spiritual follower of the monastic communities of Mount Athos, where he had previously lived as a monk himself. It is perhaps his *Tales of the Hermetical Life* which most encapsulate his ascetic views of monastic spirituality and the life a monk should follow. While Nil was never

---

[14] Zguta, "The '*Aristotelevy vrata*,'" 3-10.

seriously threatened himself, the monk Vassian, one of his followers who was more strident in his opposition, fell victim to the law against heresy and was himself condemned to death in 1531.

Saint Maximus the Greek

The "anti-possessionists," as those who rejected the Church's acquisition of material wealth came to be called, were strengthened by the arrival of a likeminded Greek theologian at the Kremlin court, Saint Maximus the Greek (1475-1556). Maximus was sent by the Patriarch of Constantinople at the request of the Grand Prince Vasily III to work with Greek texts from the Bible and other religious tracts. He did so by translating them into Latin, since he had little knowledge of Old Church Slavonic or the vernacular Russian of his time. Alas, this process resulted in errors that crept into the Slavic translations which were made from these Latin texts, introducing various canonical and liturgical other errors, which would have dire implications for Church unity when corrections were contemplated later.

Maximus was not only an anti-possessionist, but he also rejected attempts to establish or grant the Russian Church autocephaly. If this was not enough to make him undesirable at the Kremlin, Grand Prince Vasily also resented Maximus's refusal to accept the validity of his divorce from his childless first wife, Solominia Saburova, and second marriage to Princess Elena Glinskaia, who successfully bore him children. The Council of 1525 condemned Maximus's views and exiled him first to the Monastery of Saint Joseph of Volokolamsk, then, in 1532, to the Otroch Monastery at Tver, and finally, in 1553, to the Trinity Monastery of Saint Sergei, at Sergiev Posad, near Moscow, where he died. He left copious writings in Slavonic, which he eventually mastered, some of which praised the spirituality and asceticism of the heretic and ascetic renegade from Roman Catholicism Gerolamo Savonarola, who ruled Florence before being overthrown and burned at the stake in 1498.[15]

---

[15] Maksim Grek, *Tvoreniia* (Sviato-Troitskaia, Sergieva Lavra, 1996), 128-133.

Tsar Ivan the Terrible and the Martyrdom of the Innocents

The Council of 1553-54, over which Metropolitan Makarius presided, was initiated by Vasily III's son and successor, Ivan IV (r. 1553-1584), known more popularly and notoriously as the Ivan "the Terrible." As we have seen, it once and for all condemned the Judaizing heresy and found dissident clerics guilty, as many churchmen desired. Nonetheless, Ivan IV's conduct at the council bore witness to the oppression that the murderous tsar was beginning to exert over not only his people in general but the Church in particular. Metropolitan Athanasius, who succeeded Makarius, only resisted Ivan for two years before retiring to the Chudov Monastery. Athanasius, in turn, was succeeded in 1566 by Herman of Kazan, who lasted a mere two days, before his opposition led to his banishment. He was then succeeded by Saint Philip II (1507-1569), who bore the brunt of the tsar's rage and paid the ultimate price for his opposition. Philip had been abbot of the great Solovetsky Monastery, on an island in the White Sea, from which he, nonetheless, played a major role in the politics of Church and State.

The Solovetsky Monastery

The Solovetsky Monastery had been first established in 1436 by the monks Saints Herman (d. 1479) and Zosima (d. 1478), following another monk, Savvaty, who had first built a hermitage there in 1429. By the first half of the sixteenth century, it had also come to serve as a political prison and place of exile for Muscovy, a purpose for which it would later be used by both tsars and Soviets.

Saint Philip, the future Metropolitan, arrived at Solovetsky in 1538. Born to a great boyar family as Fedor Kolychev, he became first a monk and then, in 1548, its abbot. In 1566, he became a bishop and then Metropolitan of Moscow. In that office, he increasingly opposed the tsar, whose barbarity increased over time. When Philip refused a benediction to Ivan's ruthless enforcers – known as *oprichniki* after the state-within-a-state the tsar had founded – the tsar ordered his exile. He was removed to the Otroch Monastery in Tver, where Maximus the Greek had been imprisoned before him. The fury of the tsar did not abate, however, and in

December 1569, he was strangled by the *oprichnik* Maliuta Skuratov, whose name was already a byword for cruelty.

This order of execution had been issued directly by Ivan, and included the execution of Philip's beloved nephew, whose head was presented to the metropolitan just before his own murder. Philip was not the only prominent ecclesiastic to me such a fate. Saint Cornelius, Abbot of the Pskov Monastery of the Caves, was also cruelly martyred. Falling into a rage during his visitation there, Ivan the Terrible personally bludgeoned the monk with the cross the latter was carrying while in procession to greet the tsar. It is said that Ivan himself felt that his rage had allowed him to go too far and, recognizing the gravity of the sin he had just committed, personally carried the martyred Cornelius to the cathedral and did penance for his crime. Such murderous fits of rage, followed by a genuine if short-lived penitence, characterized much of Ivan the Terrible's life, the most tragic culmination of which was his murder of his own son Prince Ivan in 1581. That act sealed the ultimate extinction of his own dynastic line.

Establishment of the Patriarchate of Moscow

In 1589, in the reign of Ivan's successor Fedor I (r. 1584-1598), the metropolitan see of Moscow was elevated to a new Patriarchate, equal in status to that of Constantinople, Antioch, Jerusalem, and Alexandria. The new tsar was weak willed and poorly suited to ruling, so the diplomacy was left to his brother-in-law, the boyar Boris Godunov, who had married Fedor's sister Irina. The other eastern Patriarchs desperately needed Moscow's economic subsidies, since their ecclesiastical seats were in the Ottoman Empire, and soon granted their consent. The Metropolitan of Moscow, Saint Job (died 1607), became Russia's first Patriarch of the Russian Orthodox Church. His patriarchal residence was established in the Kremlin, in a massive building with Byzantine features, adjacent to the Church of the Twelve Apostles. A council held in Constantinople in 1590 confirmed this new status, and at another one, held in 1593, the four other Orthodox Patriarchs ratified this, with the support of some 42 bishops from the Orthodox world.[16]

---

[16] Ilarion, *Pravoslavie*, Vol. I (Moscow, 2016), p. 147.

While the other patriarchs enjoyed great historical prestige, all but the Patriarch of Moscow were now Ottoman subjects. Only Muscovy was now a truly independent Orthodox Christian power. Appealing to this fact of history and its ruling family's links to the Byzantine imperial dynasty, it now saw the culmination of the "Third Rome" doctrine, which proclaimed it the bulwark and protector of Orthodox Christianity and its adherents everywhere.

The Councils of Brest

A series of councils were held in Brest, in the Roman Catholic Polish-Lithuanian Commonwealth, which strove for the reunification of Orthodoxy and Roman Catholicism, in 1590-1596, despite great Orthodox opposition. The councils were happy to preserve the Eastern liturgy. Theological and liturgical inroads from both Protestantism and Latin Rite Catholicism were excluded. An acceptance of papal authority over the Kievan metropolia met with determined opposition among the Orthodox faithful, both clerical and lay. On the very day the final Council of Brest concluded, an opposing council declared those bishops who had supported this accord deposed. This, in turn, led to even great opposition by those favoring union, who appealed to King Sigismund of Poland, a devout Roman Catholic. He also supported the accord and allowed the rift between the Orthodox faithful and those advocating an acceptance of the new "Uniate" standpoint to persist. Such works as *Threnos* or *Lamentations of the Church of the East*, by Meletius Smotrytsky (c.1577-1633), Archbishop of Polotsk and later Metropolitan of Kiev, document the consternation caused by this schism, but he himself eventually accepted the Uniate position and ended his days as Archbishop of Hierapolis, a titular Roman Catholic see in Phrygia, in what is now Turkey.

Acceptance was not smooth, however. Imposition of the Uniate position by another archbishop of Polotsk, Josaphat Kuntsevych (1580-1623) led to violent resistance, and in November 1623 he was assassinated in Vitebsk, his corpse thrown into the River Dvina. The authorities responded quickly and some one hundred townspeople were executed.[17] Kuntsevych was canonized by Pope Pius IX in 1867, at a time when the

---

[17] Ibid., p. 79.

Papacy's territorial domains in Italy were targeted for inclusion by the new Italian nation state.

The Time of Troubles and the Tribulations of the Church

With the extinction of Rurikid dynasty upon Tsar Fedor I's death in 1598, a Time of Troubles (*smutnoe vremia*) fell over Muscovy as boyars, pretenders to the throne, and Muscovy's powerful Polish and Swedish neighbors vied for control. Boris Godunov, Fedor's brother-in-law, became Tsar, but was challenged by a pretender, a monk who assumed the identity of Ivan IV's youngest son Dmitri, who had died in suspicious circumstances in 1591. Boris was widely blamed for his murder but may well have been innocent. Dmitri, however, won the backing of Poland and led an army that took Moscow shortly after Boris's death in 1605 and briefly placed Dmitri on the throne.

Under Dmitri, Metropolitan Ignatii of Riazan (1605-06) briefly became patriarch, only to be deposed by the boyar Vasily Shuishky who himself became Tsar (r. 1606-1610) after Dmitri was overthrown and killed by the Muscovite populace. Metropolitan Hermogenes of Kazan then became patriarch. Vasily himself was soon overthrown and Patriarch Hermogenes was locked away in the Kremlin's Monastery of the Miracles when the Poles again occupied Moscow. Ignatii then returned but fled with the Poles when they were ejected from Moscow in 1612. In exile, he was received into the Greek rite of the Catholic Church and appointed Abbot of the Holy Trinity Monastery in Vilnius.

With the selection of the sixteen year-old Michael Romanov to become Tsar in 1613, the Time of Troubles came to an end. The Romanov family had held high office under Ivan IV. Michael's great-aunt Anastasia was Ivan's beloved first wife. Michael's father, the boyar Fedor Romanov, had supported Boris Godunov's election, but Godunov believed him to be too powerful and obliged him and Michael's mother to take holy orders. Fedor, now known by the religious name Philaret, was confined to a monastery in the Russian north. The pretender Dmitri, however, released him and made him Metropolitan of Rostov. In 1609 the second pretender claiming Dmitri's identity has him named patriarch in the limited area under his control, but in 1610 the resurgent Poles took him prisoner. After his release in 1619, upon the formal peace treaty, Philaret returned to Moscow, was canonically confirmed in the office of Patriarch, and became Russia's de facto ruler until his death in 1633. At no time before or since has the patriarch's power rivalled that of the Russian ruler more than it did then.

As part of the political settlement, Kiev, along with most Russian territory west of the Dniepr river, remained under Polish rule and exposed to the influences of Latin Christendom. In 1633, the new Metropolitan of Kiev, Pyotr Mogila (in Ukrainian Mohyla, died 1646), undertook a major revival of Saint Sophia Cathedral and founded a new theological college under Rector Isaiah Kozlovsky (died 1651). Latin now became the medium of instruction, following a Scholastic model inspired by Thomas Aquinas's magisterial *Summa Theologica* (1265-74).

Kozlovsky produced his own catechism, his famous *Profession of the Orthodox Faith*, which sought to remedy the perceived errors of the catechism promoted by the Patriarch of Constantinople. By the mid seventeenth century, however, the Kievan Church began to look toward Moscow for guidance. After Ukraine made a pledge of allegiance to Russia under the Union of Pereyaslav, in 1654, the theological bonds grew closer, and were solidified when Poland surrendered Kiev back to Russian rule in 1667. The metropolitan see of Kiev was united with Moscow under Patriarch Joachim (1621-90) in 1685. This arrangement was confirmed by the Patriarch of Constantinople the following year. Orthodox Russia, as Muscovy and its extended territories now came to be known, was reunited.

The Reforms of Patriarch Nikon

The ascension of Metropolitan Nikon of Novgorod (1605-81) as Patriarch in 1652 heralded major reforms within the Russian Orthodox Church. These reforms had great political as well as spiritual implications. Of humble rural origins, Nikon had become a monk at the Solovetsky Monastery. Through an acquaintanceship with Michael Romanov's son and heir Alexei (r. 1645-1676), however, he rapidly rose through the church hierarchy and amassed a considerable degree of political influence. During the tsar's campaigns against Poland, Nikon ruled from Moscow as "grand sovereign" in 1654-55. Yet his political and ecclesiastical stars fell, when in 1658, he lost favor with the Russian autocrat and was exiled to the New Jerusalem or Resurrection Monastery, near Moscow. This monastery had been founded by Nikon, in 1656, on a site where the River Istra and the heights above it recalled, at least in his mind's eye, the River Jordan and Jerusalem itself. Two years later, when the ecclesiastical council of the Church forced his removal from the patriarchal throne, the Patriarch accused its members of forming "a synagogue of Satan" and "a coven of demons."[18] Eight years later, another council, with the Patriarchs of Alexandria and Antioch presiding, confirmed his deposition.

Nikon's reforms roiled his turbulent patriarchate. Among these reforms, which began at a church council summoned in 1654, were the removal of elements of liturgy and religious custom, as well as the correction of contradictions in canon law, which had erroneously crept into Church usage over the centuries. Nikon sought a return to original Greek canonical forms. Such popular ecclesiastical figures as Bishop Paul of Kolomna and Archpriests John Neronov and Avvakum Petrov, however, vigorously opposed him, even decrying the reforms as the cause of a veritable schism within the Russian Orthodox Church. Nikon responded by stripping Paul of his bishopric and banishing him to the far north. In 1656, Paul was murdered. To many of the those who rejected the reforms, Paul was a martyr. Surviving opposition, and a new style of icon painting that evinced Western "Roman Catholic" influences, some prelates turned against Nikon, accusing him of sacrilege, even heresy. Despite Nikon's eventual deposition, his reforms remained in force. Those unwilling to accept them formed a schismatic community that came to be known as "Old Believers," who were subjected to ruthless persecution.

Today it is commonly held that both Nikon and the Tsar undertook these reforms under an erroneous assumption – that the books written in Church Slavonic were full of errors because, what they contained was at variance from the latest Greek books in print in Venice. In fact, it was these modern Greek books which were at variance with the original Greek texts, not the Church Slavonic translations. The scholars who used these new Greek texts as their sources, largely based in Kiev, were also deeply

---

[18] Ibid., 148.

influenced by Roman Catholicism. Indeed, one of them adopted Catholicism and Islam at different times in his life. Many Old Believers were not put off by the need to purify church malpractice, such as the reading of two texts simultaneously to shorten the liturgy, but rather by the ways in which the reforms were carried out, which included violence and the destruction of ancient texts and icons.[19]

There can be little doubt that many Old Believers fatally overreacted in ways that led them to fall outside the bounds of the canonical church.

The most violent opposition to Nikon's reforms took place at the Solovetsky Monastery, from 1667 to 1676. Tsar Alexei's forces besieged and captured the monastery and executed the survivors. Archpriest Avvakum was burned at the stake – not as a heretic but because of the insults he had hurled at the tsar – and many unreconciled schismatics committed mass suicide by burning their churches around them in extraordinary acts of self-immolation. Others survived in the peripheries of the Russian Empire or, later, in emigration, where they still practice their faith today. As violent persecutions subsided, Old Believers within Russia remained subject to civil disabilities until 1905. With limited access to many roles in Russian society, some gravitated toward mercantile enterprises, with notable figures amassing great fortunes.

---

[19] N. F. Kapterev, *Patriarkh Nikon i Tsar Aleksei Mikhailovich* (Moscow: Izd. Spaso-Preobrazhenskogo, Valaamskogo Monastyria, 1996), 6.

Chapter 5

The Beginning of
the "Babylonian Captivity"

Peter the Great and Russian Orthodoxy

Tsar Peter the Great (r. 1682-1725) has gone down in history as a modernizing autocrat who used despotic methods to bring Russia into the modern world, drawing inspiration from Western European technology and knowhow. Yet he was also a son of Russian Orthodoxy. On his Grand Embassy to Western Europe in 1698, when he travelled "incognito" to various capitals, one of his most significant acts was to open a Russian Orthodox chapel at the Russian Embassy in London. Ever since, there has been a Russian Orthodox place of worship there, though it has moved to a variety of locations and expanded into a multiplicity of parishes.

Peter also devoted a considerable amount of financial largesse to embellishing in both spiritual and architectural terms his new Western capital of St. Petersburg, founded in 1703, from land wrested away from Protestant Sweden and its warrior King Charles XII.

The Cathedral of Saints. Peter and Paul, St. Petersburg

Among the first of Peter's great ecclesiastical projects was the construction of the imposing High Baroque Saints Peter and Paul Cathedral, which served the Peter and Paul Fortress. The first church on the site was built of wood, painted to look like brick and surmounted by three spires. This structure was replaced by a far more majestic edifice, rising to a height of 122 meters (400 feet), created by the Italian architect Domenico Trezzini in 1712-33. With its wide windows admitting outdoor light, three principal aisles, and interior informed by Corinthian capitals over faux-marble piers, this *chef d'œuvre* clearly looks more to Rome than Moscow or anywhere else in Russia for church architectural inspiration. Yet the interior boasts a gilded iconostasis by Ivan Zarudnyi, the individual icons of which are said to be by the Moscow icon painter Andrei Pospelov. [20] Lightening severely damaged the cathedral in 1756, but another great Italian architect Francesco Bartolommeo Rastrelli, son of the Florentine architect and sculptor Carlo Bartolommeo Rastrelli, carried out its reconstruction. The latter had been invited, with his family, by Peter the Great to Russia, who had been impressed by his work at Versailles, which the tsar had seen on his visit to the French court.

The Alexander Nevsky Monastery

Peter the Great also commissioned the great Alexander Nevsky Monastery (*Lavra*) in his new capital. It was dedicated to the memory of the thirteenth century Russian warrior-saint who, with the assistance of the Mongols, resisted the onslaught of both Catholic Sweden and the Teutonic Knights in the 1240s. Work on the monastery commenced in 1710, based on designs by Trezzini. First to be completed was its Church of the Annunciation, consecrated in 1724. The Bavarian architect Theodor Schwertfeger completed the project, but much of his work later proved structurally unsound and had to be rebuilt under the leading Russian architect of that period, Ivan Starov, in 1776-90. He, too, used a Western European Baroque design, but with neoclassical elements, evident in his use of pilasters, which were the height of fashion in Paris at that time. Peter the Great thus Westernized not only the government of the Church, but its very architectural fabric. [21]

The Petrine Reforms and the Abolition of the Patriarchate

The death of Patriarch Adrian (1627-1700) allowed Peter the Great to let the office to fall into abeyance. Thus began a period that the twentieth-century theologian and priest Georges Florovsky (1893-1979) called the

---

[20] Neil Kent, *St Petersburg* (London, 2017), p. 172.
[21] Ibid, 172.

"Babylonian Captivity."[22] Peter, the Westernizing Tsar, looked to Europe for inspiration on administrative, technological, and cultural levels, and entertained an Erastian view of the Church, according to which the head of state should hold sway over its administration and supervision. In 1720, just before his assumption of the title of Emperor, Peter established the Most Holy Synod, an ecclesiastical college that would administer the affairs of the Russian Orthodox Church. Three years later, the Patriarchate, which had been dormant for over twenty years, was formally abolished. The validity of this action was confirmed by the patriarchs of Constantinople and Antioch, both of whose sees remained under the authority of the Ottoman Sultan, and therefore continued to be dependent upon financial remittances from Russia and thus the Tsar's good will.

The Synod was personified as "the sister in Christ" of the Patriarchs, though its members were, of course, all men. It would eventually be accommodated in a palatial edifice, completed in 1834 by the Italian architect Carlo Rossi. In the present era, it is now the seat of Russia's Constitutional Court and the Boris Yeltsin Presidential Library, but also contains apartments to accommodate meetings of the Russian patriarch and president.

By abolishing the Patriarchate, Peter ensured that state secular power would have no powerful rival in the religious sphere. Philaret had been Russia's de facto ruler while his son reigned. Nikon merely overreached, and in response Russia's autocratic secular ruler became the "defender of the Church," on the model of his peers in the Scandinavian countries and Great Britain. Peter was supported in this by the theologian and Bishop Theophan Prokopovich of Pskov (1681-1736), who later became Archbishop of Novgorod. Theophan provided the theological and practical justification for this Erastian view. His treatises, which supported the Emperor's position, included *A Word on the Power and Honor of the Tsar* and *The Truth of the Monarch's Will.* Of equal importance, his *Ecclesiastical Regulation* warned of the dangers of having a single ecclesiastical figure at the head of the Church who could seek to rival the tsar and thwart his rule. Addenda of 1722 put further constraints upon monasteries, especially in urban areas, and, in particular, on contemplative

[22] G. Florovskij, *Vie della teologia russa* (Genoa, 1987), p. 74.

orders, which the Tsar – like other eighteenth-century European monarchs – came to perceive as expending financial resources without contributing anything concrete in return. In consequence, few new monasteries were founded during the later Petrine period and the properties of some were confiscated.

Peter's death in 1725 did not reverse the trend. From 1730, there was a prohibition on the acquisition of new monastic lands.[23] Beginning in 1734, access to the monastic vocation became highly restricted and only permitted for widowed priests and retired soldiers. In consequence, the monastic population declined by forty percent over the period 1724-38.

Various prelates of the Church opposed these drastic innovations. Among these was Saint Dimitri of Rostov (1651-1709), who condemned Caesaropapism, that is, the union of the secular and political power under the Emperor. Dmitri had studied at the Theological Academy of Kiev, where Prokopovich had been in charge, and greatly valued monastic spiritual life. As he wrote, "The only thing necessary is to incline the mind towards God, to descend into the depths of oneself, and this is something which may be done anywhere."[24]

But these voices were crying in the wilderness. Theophan was appointed head of the Holy Synod. First, in cooperation with Peter the Great and later with the Empress Anna, his half-niece and eventual successor (r. 1730-1740), opponents of his church policy were removed from their ecclesiastical positions and exiled to remote monasteries. Within a generation, opposition to the so-called Petrine reforms were effectively crushed.

After the accession of Empress Elisabeth (daughter of Peter I, reigned 1741-1762), who was a pious adherent of Russian Orthodoxy, many churches were constructed. These included St. Petersburg's Church of the Resurrection, popularly known as the Smolny Cathedral, built in 1748-1764. It was built by Francesco Bartolommeo Rastrelli, on a site where tar for naval construction was stored. Elisabeth also established there one of Europe's finest schools for girls, specifically for daughters of

---

[23] I. Chistovich, *Feofan Prokopovich i ego vremia* (St. Petersburg, 1868), p. 714.

[24] S. Dimitri di Rostov, "L'intimo del cuore," in *Caritone di Valamo. 'Artem della preghiera* (Torino, 1980), pp. 46-48.

the nobility, including studies in mathematics and physics as well as in religion and other subjects considered more suitable for young ladies. Unlike so many other ecclesiastical buildings of its vintage, it drew upon ancient Russian inspiration, with its truncated apse, onion domes, and Christmas cake stucco decorations. By contrast, the Saint Nicholas Naval Cathedral, situated across the city on the Kriukov Canal, is late Baroque in style, with playful decoration more characteristic of the French Rococo than anything traditionally Russian. Designed by Savva Chevakinsky and built in 1753-1762, it is characterized by imperious Corinthian porticos, which adorn each side of this cruciform church. Typical for a northern Russian church, it contains two sanctuaries, one below for the winter and one above for the summer months, both of which are richly adorned by lustrous icons.

Ecclesiastical Reaction and the Revival of Monastic Life to marry Peter III

By the early 1740s, an ecclesiastical reaction found considerable support among the nobility as well as clerics. The decline in the state of the monasteries, by then populated by a geriatric monastic order on the verge of extinction, made it incumbent upon the Holy Synod to reopen many monasteries and young novice monks from all social classes were once again admitted.

This reprieve would last only a generation. The accession to the throne of the Prussian-influenced Emperor Peter III (reigned briefly in 1762 before his murder in a coup d'état) again imposed severe constraints on the monasteries, an approach made even more stringent under his consort and successor, the German-born Empress Catherine II, "the Great" (reigned 1762-96), who had converted to Orthodoxy to marry Peter IIII.

Catherine, whose policies mirrored those of European "enlightened despots," implemented early in her reign a massive confiscation of monastic lands. Some 469 monasteries out of a total of 881 throughout Russia were suppressed. The monastic population was more than halved, reduced from some 11,000 monks and nuns to 5,450.[25] Metropolitan Arseny (Matseyevich) of Rostov (1697-1772) objected vociferously, only to be removed from his office and exiled to a remote monastery, by order of the Most Holy Synod at the command by the Empress. This failed to silence him, and he was later incarcerated in the Fortress of Reval (now Tallinn, in Estonia), where he died. He was canonized by the Russian Orthodox Church in 2000.

Establishment and Development of Religious Academies

While monasteries were suppressed, the establishment and development of religious academies – albeit under strict governmental supervision – was encouraged. As early as 1685, an academy of Slavonic, Greek, and Latin was founded in Moscow, serving the needs of ecclesiastical training and made possible by the generosity of two Cephalonian Greek brothers, Ioannikios and Sophronious Leichoudes (Likhud, in Russian). This institution eventually became the Moscow Theological Academy. A modern statue (2007) memorializing the founding brothers can be found in Moscow today.

By the early 1720s, other schools and seminaries had opened their doors in St. Petersburg, Nizhny Novgorod, Kharkov, Tver, Kazan, Vyatka, Kholmogory, Kolomna, Ryazan, Vologda, and Pskov. Over the course of the eighteenth century, some 150 religious institutes were created. This number more than doubled, to some 340, during the reign of Tsar Alexander I (r. 1801-1825). This figure included the three theological academies – in Kiev, Moscow, and St. Petersburg, – as well as 39 major seminaries, 128 minor ones, and 170 parish schools.[26] Kiev's theological academy had the greatest influence, for it trained most future Church leaders. Latin was the medium of instruction, and the curriculum was heavily influenced by Jesuit instruction common in Western Europe. For this and other reasons, the influence of Roman Catholic academic life on

---

[25] Andronik [Trubachev], A. A. Bovkalo, and A. Fedorov, "Monastyri i monashestvo, 1700-1998 gg.," in *Pravoslavnaia entsiklopediia: Russkaia Pravoslavnaia Tserkov* (Moscow, 1997), 327-328.

[26] M. Kozlov, "Dukhovnoe obrazovanie XVII-XX gg.," in *Pravoslavnaia entsiklopediia: Russkaia Pravoslavnaia Tserkov* (Moscow, 1997), pp. 409-412.

Russian Orthodox theological teaching reached its zenith during this period.

Saint Tikhon of Zadonsk

One leading spiritual and theological figure of this period was St. Tikhon of Zadonsk (1724-1783). Among his most noted works were *The Spiritual Treasury, Gathered from the World* (1770) and *On True Christianity* (1776). Following in the tradition of the early Church father Saint John Chrysostom, Archbishop of Constantinople in the late fourth century AD, Tikhon combined eloquence with an ascetic lifestyle and was known as a "wonder worker." Perhaps more than any other ecclesiastical figure of his time, Tikhon, who served as Bishop of Voronezh, emphasized the importance of the Bible and its teachings as a rich reservoir of Christian moral teaching and spirituality, above and beyond its use in the liturgy.

Not all monks received a literary and theological education of such depth. This excluded them from higher ecclesiastical positions, and they generally worked in monasteries in which hospitals, military barracks, and the poor were accommodated, and from which they ordinarily were not permitted to depart.[27] Only in the nineteenth century did the academic center of gravity in Russia begin to shift away from Kiev to Moscow. When this happened, Latin began to lose its linguistic hegemony in ecclesiastical circles and Russian again became the language of theological discourse, while patristic studies came to dominate. By then, the caste-like nature of the clergy also began to loosen up. During the eighteenth century and into the middle of the nineteenth, the priesthood and monastic life had been rigidly subject to the secular authorities and informed by family background, rather than personal religious vocation, with generally only the sons and sons-in-law of priests and deacons eligible for ordination or monastic orders.

Missionary Work of the Clergy

Despite the restrictions imposed upon the clergy and their activities, missionary work continued apace, especially eastwards into Siberia. In this context, Saint Innocent of Irkutsk (1680-1731) was of special

---

[27] Chistovich, *Feofan Prokopovich*, 714-715.

importance in bringing pagan Asian peoples into the Orthodox fold. Scion of a noble family that had settled in the vicinity of Chernigov, in today's Ukraine, he attended the Kiev Theological Academy, before being transferred to the Alexander Nevsky Lavra in St. Petersburg. When Archimandrite Hilarion, the Russian emissary to China, died in 1717, Innocent was assigned to take his place. Denied permission to cross the border by the Chinese authorities, he was instead invested as bishop of the new diocese of Irkutsk and Nerchinsk, the boundaries of which were later extended to include Yakutsk and Ilimsk. He laid the groundwork that opened the way for Saint Herman to cross the Bering Straits a century later and bring Russian Orthodoxy to Alaska.

Westwards, too, proselytizing activities were carried out among the Uniates, many of whom came under Russian rule after the partitions of Poland in 1772, 1793, and 1795. Especially of note in this regard was the work of Archbishop Georgy Konissky (1717-95), who brought at least 100,000 Uniates back to the Orthodox fold. By 1784, Russian Orthodox believers numbered some 21,690,201, an increase from about 10,000,000 in 1722.[28]

Spiritual Revival, the *Philocalia*, and Saint Seraphim of Sarov

Along with increased missionary activity, a great spiritual revival began as well. During the later decades of the eighteenth century, theologians like the Greek-born Saint Nicodemus the Hagiorite (of the Holy Mountain, 1749-1809), based as a monk on Mount Athos, encouraged a spiritual revival throughout the Orthodox world. Through his writings, which included a variety of spiritual texts and were gradually disseminated throughout Russia, he would exhort the faithful to frequent holy communion, a stance that exerted a profound influence on the practice in Russia. As a result, his great theological and spiritual opus *Philocalia* (*Love of the Beautiful*), first published in Venice in 1782, became one of the most important treasure houses of Orthodox thought. Its first Church Slavonic translation appeared in 1793, and it was later published in

---

[28] V. Tsypin, "Russkaia Pravoslavnaia Tserkov v sinodal'nuiu epokhi," in *Pravoslavnaia entsiklopediia*, 132.

Russian. A vast, multivolume work, it encapsulated Orthodox wisdom from the fourth to the fifteenth centuries and, with its focus on prayer and prayerfulness, has exerted an immense influence on the Orthodox faithful worldwide ever since.

Saint Seraphim of Sarov (1754–1833) was another highly important figure of the era. He stressed the importance of contemplative prayer not only for clerics, monks, and nuns, but for the laity as well. His own life bore witness to the stress he placed on personal devotion: for 25 years he was a hieromonk living in seclusion before entering the Monastery of Sarov, where he became a central figure of popular Orthodox spirituality.

The Baptism of Saint Prince Vladimir, Viktor Vasnetsov (1890)

Cathedral of the Dormition in the Monastery of the Caves, **Kiev**

Saint Sergei of Radonezh, **by Sergei Kirillov (1993)**

Transfiguration, icon by Theophanes the Greek (15th century)

Virgin of Vladimir, icon by Andrei Rublev (1400)

Christ the Redeemer by Andrei Rublev

Christ's Harrowing of Hell by **Dionisii** (c. 1495-96)

Saint Philip II, Metropolitan of Moscow, icon

Solovetsky Monastery

Patriarch Philaret

New Jerusalem Monastery

Alexander Nevsky Monastery, St. Petersburg

Palace of the Most Holy Synod, St. Petersburg

Saint Tikhon of Zadonsk

Saint Philaret of Moscow

Saint Nicholas of Japan   *Saint John of Kronstadt*

Davidov Pustyn Monastery of the Ascension, Novyy Byt

Metropolitan Tikhon of Moscow

Metropolitan Anthony of Sourozh

Chapter 6

Spiritual Revival and
the Threats of Secular Liberalism

Metropolitan Philaret of Moscow

By the early nineteenth century, the Holy Synod had succeeded in clawing back a considerable degree of power and autonomy. This was to a large degree secured through the efforts of Metropolitan Philaret (Drozdov) of Moscow (1782–1867). He had been elevated to the see of Moscow in 1826 and became a member of the Holy Synod. From then until his death, he held a level of authority unknown since the days of his namesake, Patriarch Philaret, in the seventeenth century.

Metropolitan Philaret succeeded in cementing a close relationship with Tsar Nicholas I (r. 1825-1855), who gave him much support. Because of this and what his enemies perceived to be illiberal views, he won the ire of the liberal opposition, not least that of the "Father of Russian Socialism" Alexander Herzen, who was hostile to monastic life and to Orthodoxy in general. In his memoirs, *My Past and Thoughts* (1870), Herzen accused the metropolitan of thanking God for the "murders," that is, the executions in 1826 of five rebel leaders of the Decembrist movement, which attempted a revolutionary transformation of Russia upon Nicholas I's succession the previous year.[29] Yet it was the same Philaret who took an active role in the emancipation of the serfs in February 1861, promulgated under Nicholas I's son and successor Tsar Alexander II (reigned 1855–81). Indeed, the metropolitan himself wrote the text of the manifesto freeing the serfs.

---

[29] A. I. Gertsen, *Byloe i dumy* (Moscow, 1958), p. 221.

Three years earlier, in 1858, Philaret had published the first translation of the Bible from Old Church Slavonic into modern Russian, an enormous labor that made the holy book accessible to a much wider portion of the Russian population than ever before. It was a massive joint undertaking by all four Russian theological academies – Moscow, St. Petersburg, Kiev, and Kazan. By the time of its publication, however, Philaret had left the Holy Synod because of a disagreement with its Chief Procurator, Count Nikolai Protasov (1798-1855), who attempted to restrict ecclesiastical autonomy. Instead, Philaret continued to devote himself to the reform of religious education in Russia. In this he followed in the footsteps of the late Tsar Nicholas I, who was keen to improve and expand education. Some of Philaret's works, such as *Colloquy between a Believer and a Skeptic on the True Doctrine of the Greco-Russian Church* (1815), contrast Orthodox beliefs with those of Roman Catholicism, while his *Christian Catechism* (1823) elaborated the doctrines of the Orthodox faith to make them more accessible to a wider laity. He was canonized in 1994.

Our Lady of Kazan Cathedral

A major period of church and monastic construction took place during the early and middle decades of the nineteenth century. This was especially true in St. Petersburg, which saw a resurgence of cathedral building. One of Russia's greatest churches, the Cathedral of Our Lady of Kazan, was built on Nevsky Prospekt in a style evoking St. Peter's Cathedral in Rome rather than any Russian or, indeed, Orthodox church. Its architect was a former serf, Andrey Voronikhin, who had previously worked on the palace of his former owner (and perhaps father) Count Andrei Stroganov, further along on Nevsky. With its Latin cross plan, Corinthian porticos, and flanking colonnades, Our Lady of Kazan expressed the architectural tastes of Tsar Paul I, whose memorial decorates the interior nave by the principal entrance. Today a red stone by the altar delineates the spot where the martyred Tsar Nicholas II customarily stood when attending religious services. During the Soviet period it became a Museum of Atheism, but today is the mother church of the Metropolitan of St. Petersburg.

Saint Isaac's Cathedral

Even larger than the Cathedral of Our Lady of Kazan is Saint Isaac's Cathedral, also in St. Petersburg, built between 1818 to 1858 by the French Roman Catholic architect Auguste de Montferrand. It was constructed on the site of an earlier cathedral built originally by Rinaldi. Tsar Paul disliked the original structure and wanted to replace it, but only later was the cathedral finally completed after many changes of architect and style. Built in the Greek inspired neo-classical style then in fashion, its interior columns are richly decorated with cladding of a lustrous green Siberian malachite and blue lapis lazuli. Most unusual for a Russian Orthodox Church, it incorporates a stained-glass altar window imported from Bavaria, which depicts the Resurrection. Its iron and bronze work was produced by the British-owned Baird Works Foundry, which had recently been established in the imperial capital. During the Soviet period, Saint Isaac's also became a museum and technically still remains one today, though it has been used for religious services on ecclesiastical occasions. In October 2021, it was the site of the wedding of Grand Duke George of Russia, widely considered to be the heir to the throne, and only the second royal marriage in Russia since 1918.

Petr Chaadaev

Then as now, many Russians sought to undermine the authority of Russian Orthodoxy. One such virulent figure was the Russian philosopher Petr Chaadaev (1794–1856). He was a member of a Westernizing circle whose members followed Friedrich Wilhelm Joseph von Schelling and drew inspiration from "liberal enlightenment values" inspired by the French Revolution. Chaadaev was hostile to many aspects of the Russian Orthodox Church, which he perceived as backward. In particular, he criticized its refusal to condemn serfdom, its mysticism, and its quietism, all of which he contrasted with his more benign global vision of Roman Catholicism (even though the Roman Catholic Church, too, was also largely uncritical of both slavery and serfdom). It is said that he was a model for the character Chatsky, the troublesome protagonist of the famous play *Woe from Wit* (1824) by the great Russian playwright Alexander Griboyedov. Although he was declared insane by government authorities, who thought his values threatened to undermine those of the

Russian state, he nonetheless frequented the Empire's highest literary circles, especial that of that Russian literary giant Alexander Pushkin. Chaadaev's *Philosophical Letters* (1826–1831) had considerable influence among Russian intellectuals who could read French, the language in which it was written. The work further encouraged the secularization of Russia's educated classes, to the detriment of both Church and State.

Alexander Pushkin

The personality of Russia's greatest poet, Alexander Pushkin (1799–1837), was often contradictory and even tormented. On the one hand, as Metropolitan Hilarion (Alfeyev) of Volokolamsk points out, Pushkin could write a long blasphemous poem as *Gabrieliad* (1821), while on the other hand he could repent of it and go on to produce his inspirational poem *The Prophet* (1828), inspired by the sixth chapter of the Book of Isaiah in the Bible.[30] For Sergei Bulgakov, this poem made up for all. As he wrote, "Even if we did not possess any other work by Pushkin, it shines for us the eternal snow of this unique peak; we can see with complete clarity not only the sublimity of his poetic gift, but also all the stature of his vocation."[31] Indeed, this masterly poem even inspired Metropolitan Philaret to respond in the form of a poem, which may demonstrate that he understood the doubts and disbelief that battled for faith within Pushkin's soul.[32] This, in turn, inspired a riposte from Pushkin, in his poem *Stanze*:

> *In your fire the spirit reheated*
> *Has repelled the shadow of early vanity*
> *And inclines the ear to the harp of Philaret*
> *The poet with the sacred fear.*[33]

Whatever his spiritual and moral failings, Pushkin himself went to his maker as an Orthodox believer, having received confession and holy

---

[30] Ilarion, *Pravoslavie*, pp. 229-230.
[31] S. N. Bulgakov *'Zhrebyi Pushkina': Pushkin v russkoi filosofkoi kritike: konets XIX-pervaia polovina XX v.* (Moscow, 1990), p. 283.
[32] Philaret Moskovskii, 'Ne naprasno, ne sluchaino,' in A. S. Pushkin, *Sochineniia pis'ma* (St. Petersburg, 1903), pp. 435–436.
[33] A. S. Pushkin, *V chasy zabav il'prazdnoi skuki*, in Pushkin, *Polnoe sobranie sochinenii* (Moscow, 1956-58), III, p. 62.

communion on his death bed after a fatal duel. So, too, did another famous Orthodox Russian author and poet, Mikhail Lermontov (1814–41), who also died in a duel, despite Church condemnation of such "honor combats." Indeed, his writings, like those of Pushkin, are infused with strong religious feeling and are rich in Biblical allusions. One is explicitly entitled *Prayer:*

> *In the hour of the trial of life,*
> *When the heart is oppressed by sadness,*
> *A Miraculous prayer*
> *I repeat in my memory.*
> *It has the force of benediction*
> *In the harmony of words which live,*
> *And a charm in them breathes, mysterious, sacred.*[34]

This poem was later set to music by a number of Russian composers, including Mikhail Glinka, Modest Mussorgsky, and Anton Rubinstein, as well as in the West by Franz Liszt.

Perhaps Pushkin's life can best be summed up in his long poem *The Demon* (several versions 1829–39, and also set as an opera by Rubinstein), in which good unequivocally triumphs over evil.

Aleksei Komiakov

Chaadaev's views can be contrasted with those of another Russian literary and political figure of philosophical bent, Aleksei Komiakov (1804–60). A staunch founder and defender of pan-Slavism, a movement which, encouraged the fraternity of all Slavs and the celebration of Slavic traditions, he focused upon the concept of *sobornost,*' that is a symphonic harmony amongst the tsar's subjects with roots in ancient Byzantine religious and political culture. This ideology found its best expression in *There Is Only One Church* (1864), a tract which would greatly influence other pan-Slavic theologians, philosophers, and writers. It stressed the role of Russian Orthodoxy as a means of leading first the Slavic peoples and then the entire world to spiritual salvation in Christ.

---

[34] *M. Iu. Lermontov, "Molitva," in Lermontov, Izbrannye proizvedeniia* (Moscow, 1957, p. 105).

Komiakov took an interest in Anglicanism and engaged in a long correspondence with the British theologian William Palmer (1811–79), a deacon of Magdalen College, Oxford, who in 1840 made the first of several of his visits to Russia. Thus began a lengthy dialogue of the Anglican Church with the Russian Orthodox Church, which almost led to their ecclesiastical union in the early years of the twentieth century. Palmer's Erastian views on the monarch as head of the Church, as well as his rejection of adult re-baptism, as had begun to be practiced in the Greek Church in the Ottoman Empire, also found a resonance in Russian governmental and ecclesiastical circles at that time.

Fyodor Dostoyevsky and the Phenomenon of the Elder in Late Nineteenth-Century Russia

The third quarter of the nineteenth century witnessed a renaissance of monastic life in Russia. This was in part facilitated by spiritual elders of the Church, or *startsy* (singular *starets*), a leading fictional example of which is the elderly monk Zosima, from the world-famous novel by Fyodor Dostoyevsky (1821-81), *The Brothers Karamazov* (1879–80). The character is based on a real-life person, the elder Leonid (Lev) (1768-1841), a monk of the Optina Pustyn Monastery, southeast of Moscow,[35] though Saint Tikhon of Zadonsk, the Venerable Makarius, and Saint Ambrosius of Optina (1812-91) are also said to be prototypes.[36]

For Dostoyevsky, Russia's mission was to bring a pure Orthodoxy, unadulterated by Western European values, to save a wider world. This revival of an ancient Byzantine tradition could be traced back more recently to its revival by the monk Saint Paisius Velichkovsky (1722–1794), who eventually settled down at Mount Athos, then under Ottoman suzerainty, before moving to the Neamt Monastery in Moldavia, in today's Romania, also then under Ottoman suzerainty. His translation of parts of Nicodemus's compilation, the *Philokalia*, was first published in 1793, but appeared as *Dobrotoliubie,* in St. Petersburg in 1803 and was to have an immense influence on monastic life in Russia throughout the

---

[35] I. M. Kantsevich, *Optina pustyn' i ee vremia* (Jordanville, New York, 1970), pp. 131-63)
[36] Alfeev, *La Chiesa Ortodossa*, p. 244.

nineteenth century and beyond. Among the famous figures who visited these elders over the course of the nineteenth century were, besides Dostoyevsky, the great authors Nikolai Gogol and Lev Tolstoy.

Nikolai Gogol

Nikolai Gogol (1809–52) was one of Russia's most famous writers in the first half of the nineteenth century. He was especially renowned for his two greatest novels *Dead Souls* (1842) and *The Government Inspector* (1842). Full of humor and mocking the foibles of the times, these were hardly works with serious religious themes – "souls" was a term that signified a serf, not a spiritual concept. Gogol's later work, *Meditations on the Divine Liturgy*, is one of the most spiritually important works of its period. Focusing on the writings of the early fathers of the Eastern Church, it explores the spirituality and mystical treasurers of the Orthodox Communion service, relating them to Gogol's own experiences and insights. As such, it is a work of great spiritual import to this day. A troubled soul himself, Gogol, too, sought out a *starets* and carried out a pilgrimage to Jerusalem in 1848. Nonetheless, spiritual serenity largely eluded him.

Saint Ignatius Bryanchaninov

More successful in achieving peace of mind was one of the greatest spiritual leaders of this period, Saint Ignatius Bryanchaninov (1807–67). Scion of a noble family from the province of Vologda, he had fallen under the spiritual sway of Leonid of the Optina Pustyn Monastery. He is most famed for his advocacy of the so-called Jesus prayer for the faithful: *Lord Jesus Christ, Have Mercy on Us*, or similar variations. This spiritual exercise was later widely adopted not only in the Orthodox world, but throughout the Roman Catholic and Anglican Churches. Indeed, it is practiced to this day by the former Archbishop of Canterbury Rowan Williams.

Nevertheless, Ignatius was no ecumenical figure: he was highly critical of the spiritual writings of Roman Catholic saints, including Frances of Assisi, Ignatius of Loyola and Theresa of Avila. It was the medieval Saint Thomas à Kempis who most evoked his greatest opprobrium, possibly because the latter's *Imitation of Christ* (1418–27) achieved considerable popularity among the Russian nobility and threatened to woo them away from Orthodoxy. Instead, Ignatius advocated the spiritual readings of such Orthodox figures as Saint Simon the New Theologian and Saint Gregory of Sinai. Ignatius's *Paternikon,* which focuses on the spiritual writings and exercises of these saints of the Egyptian desert, soon acquired a vast readership. It should be remembered that the Saint Catherine's Monastery on the Sinai Peninsula, founded in 565 AD and dedicated to the early martyr Saint Catherine of Alexandria, was drawing increasing attention in the nineteenth century because of its wealth of manuscripts and icons. Its *Codex Sinaiticus,* from the fourth century AD, was the oldest known mostly complete manuscript of the Holy Bible. Soon made its way to Russia, as Tsar Alexander II (r. 1855-1881) was a major donor to the Monastery, but in the Soviet period Stalin sold that great book to the British Museum, where it remains to this day.

In some respects, the voice of Saint Igantius was "crying in the wilderness." For all his exhortations to adopt an ascetic way of life and eschew the worldly pleasures of "theatres, balls, cards, and other Satanic games," his message increasingly fell on deaf ears not only in the wider society, but among the clergy. Even the Orthodox monasteries of Russia, he became convinced, had fallen victim to the evil times in which he lived:

> Our monasteries are corrupt; everything is corrupt in them, and even what they signify is corrupt. The institutes of religious education are so far from the spirit of the Orthodox faith, that it is a veritable rarity that at the end of the seminary someone enters a monastery, and in the course of 50 years of the foundation of the academic theological academies, there is not one example of a person who completed his studies and entered a monastery ... Our monasteries are completely decadent.[37]

That said, Ignatius was no man of the Middle Ages and by no means rejected the benefits of empirical science. He wrote, "Nature announces God ... and the sciences, which clarify the laws of nature, even more so

---

[37] L. Sokolov, *Sviatitel' Ignatii. Ego zhzin', lichnost' i moral'no-asketicheskie vozzreniia* (Moscow, 2003), pp. 63-64.

announce God. All the grand scholars, mathematicians and scientists, such as Newton, Leibniz, Necker, were not just Deists but loved Christianity."[38]

Ignatius's deep spirituality notwithstanding, there were other devout spiritual leaders who took exception to some of his teachings. One such personage was Bishop Theophan the Recluse (1815–94). Their disagreements might seem largely theological, the former having the belief that angels and the spirit possess corporeal elements, the latter only spiritual ones. However, in reality these differences were more defined by temperament: Ignatius was academically fastidious, while Theophan took a more paraphrastic approach, which sought contemporary relevance over accuracy, especially when it related to literary translations, not least that of the *Philokalia*. In particular, Theophan was keen for the laity to participate regularly in the services and sacraments of the Church. This, in his view, required the introduction of a modern simplified form of Old Church Slavonic rather than a modern translation into Russian, which he felt would diminish rather than enhance the language.

Apostate Seminarians

Hostility to Orthodoxy was not only to be found outside the Church. Sometimes, the greatest enemies of the Church came from within its bosom. The novelist Nikolai Pomialovsky (1835-63), for example, came from a clerical family and had been a seminarian before turning his back on the Church. His *Sketches from a Seminary* gave a notorious inside view of the decadence he claimed to have found there. He eventually worked with radical poet and literary critic Nikolai Nekrasov and revolutionary philosopher Nikolai Chernyshevsky. The latter was also from a clerical family as well as a former seminarian. Both were connected to the radical journal, originally founded by Pushkin, *Sovremennik* (*The Contemporary*). Pomialovsky was condemned to penal servitude in 1864 and then exiled to Siberia in 1872. He died there, but left a literary legacy which would eventually be taken up by the revolutionary writer Maksim Gorky.

Without doubt the most famous of apostate seminarians was Joseph Djugashvili, known by his revolutionary alias Stalin, whose life is

---

[38] Ibid., p. 66.

beyond the scope of this book, but who wrought immense damage upon the Church in the second quarter of the twentieth century.

Missionary Work to the Borders of the Empire and Beyond

Over the course of the nineteenth century, Russian Orthodox missionaries brought the faith to the four corners of the Russian Empire and beyond. The Orthodox cross was even planted on the uninhabited Arctic island of Svalbard, 650 (1,050 kilometers) miles from the North Pole, where Russian hunters had first arrived in the late seventeenth century. In the West, Orthodoxy made major inroads in Finland, then a Grand Duchy ruled by the tsar, and in the Baltic region, where Joseph Semashko (1789-1868), the Metropolitan of Vilnius and Lithuania, secured reunification of the Uniate Church with Orthodoxy. Semashko had first been ordained as a Roman Catholic priest but later converted to Orthodoxy and overcame many obstacles in order to return the Uniates to the Orthodox fold. The process to canonize him is ongoing at this moment. In 1840, an Orthodox diocese was also established in Warsaw, in staunchly Roman Catholic Poland. Most major cities in these regions, including Tallinn (Revel), Helsinki, and Warsaw, all received large and imposing Russian Orthodox Cathedrals in this era. Additionally, a law of the Russian Empire required that children of mixed marriages involving one Orthodox partner be baptized Orthodox.

Orthodox proselytizing also reached faraway indigenous peoples. Saint Herman of Alaska (1751-1836), considered by many to be the patron saint of that American state, left the Valaam Monastary, on an island on Lake Ladoga northeast of St Petersburg, to take up missionary work there. The Danish explorer Vitus Bering, who acted in Russian service, had discovered Alaska in 1741, and Russia had taken sovereignty over it. Russian fur trappers followed in his wake, and it eventually became clear to the authorities in St. Petersburg that missionaries were needed not only for the Aleutian natives, over 7,000 of whom were baptized, but for Russians whose behavior was far from commendable. Russian churches remain in Alaska to this day.

Missionary activities in the Far East were also carried out in countries well beyond Russia's borders. Saint Nicholas (Kasatkin) of Japan (1836-1912), played a major role in this arduous endeavor. Converts whom he brought to Orthodoxy included not only Siberian tribesmen, like the Turkic speaking Tungus and Chukchi, but the Inuit of Alaska before moving on to Japan. Saint Nicholas was first appointed chaplain at the Russian consulate in Hakodate, on Hokkaido Island, where it is said he converted a samurai warrior and Shinto priest who had been sent to kill him. He became the first bishop of the Orthodox Church of Japan, having first been invested as Bishop of Reval (Tallinn) – a city which he never visited – in 1880. The following year, the Orthodox Cathedral of the Resurrection, in Tokyo, was consecrated. Although nominally under the umbrella of the Russian Orthodox Church, the Japanese Orthodox community functioned largely autonomously, an especially valuable status when throughout the Russo-Japanese, War in 1904-1905, it served the spiritual needs of not only the Japanese faithful but some 70,000 Russian prisoners-of-war. As a Russian subject, however, Saint Nicholas ceased to serve liturgy during that period, as he was unwilling to pray for a Japanese victory and yet careful not to offend Japanese loyalties. After the war, missionary activity in Japan increased and, in 1907 Nicholas became Archbishop of Japan. By 1912, there were some 31,984 Japanese Russian Orthodox faithful served by some 265 churches and 41 priests.

Saint Nicholas was succeeded by Metropolitan Sergei (Tikhomirov). After his death in 1945, and the brief military conflict between the Soviet Union and Japan which concluded the Second World War, communion between the Russian Orthodox Church in Japan and Moscow was broken. There was also a dispute over which ecclesiastical jurisdiction could claim the Japanese Church.[39] This rift would take many years to heal and was only bridged in 1970, when the autonomy of the Japanese Orthodox Church was recognized, albeit under the Moscow Patriarchate. Today there are some 100,000 faithful, most of whom are Japanese, served by three dioceses and 150 parishes.[40]

---

[39] Ilya Kharin, *After Nicholas. Self-Realisation of the Japanese Orthodox Church, 1912-1956* (Gloucester, 2014).

[40] Alfeev, *La Chiesa Ortodossa*, p. 338.

The first Russian Orthodox missionaries to China arrived in the late seventeenth century, only to find themselves in confrontation at the Ching court with Roman Catholic Jesuits. Nevertheless, the first formal Orthodox mission to Beijing took place in 1717, although its development really only prospered between 1896 and 1931 under Archimandrite, then Metropolitan, Innocent (Figurovsky). Still, calamity was to strike during the Boxer Rebellion of 1905, when 222 Chinese Orthodox faithful were tortured and executed by the rebels, who sought to wipe out both Christian and European influence. Order was quickly restored by the major powers, including Russia, and with the advent of the Chinese Republic in 1911 matters significantly improved. By 1918, there were some 10,000 Chinese Orthodox believers. Russian émigrés who sought refuge in China after the Russian Revolution considerably augmented their numbers so that by the advent of the Second World War, there were no fewer than a hundred Russian Orthodox churches in China.

After the successful communist takeover of China under Mao Zedong in 1949, most Russians in China fled elsewhere, especially to Australia and the United States. Saint John (Maximovich) of Shanghai and San Francisco (1896–1966) was extremely important in this context, leading many of his flock to the Philippines in 1949. Saint Jonah (Pokrovsky, 1888–1925) of Manchuria was also of considerable significance. He himself had suffered grievously under the Bolsheviks before being freed by White forces during the Russian Civil War. Similarly, life was difficult for believers in the new communist China, though some freedom was granted in 1957. During the Cultural Revolution of the 1960s, however, the Chinese Orthodox Church suffered dreadfully, as did other religious communities. Churches, their inventory, and even their cemeteries, were desecrated or destroyed. To this day, the Orthodox Church in China has not recovered to its pre-communist level, even if it there are some thirteen parishes in the country. Orthodoxy has, however, taken root in other eastern Asian countries, such as Thailand, the Koreas, Mongolia, and Vietnam.

The Russian Orthodox Church also expanded its mission to the south, in particular, to the North Caucasus. In 1783 – the year Crimea was annexed by the Russian Empire – the Treaty of Georgievsk accorded

Russia a protectorate over Christian Georgia, whose ruler feared conquest by Shiite Islamic Persia. When King George XII, who reigned over Georgia, died in 1801, the Russian Emperor Paul I annexed the country outright. Shortly thereafter, the new tsar Alexander I incorporated it fully into the Russian Empire as a province, with the Georgian crown prince and his family detained in St. Petersburg. In the wake of these political events, in 1811, the Georgian Orthodox Church was subsumed under the Moscow Patriarchate as an exarchate.

Across the Bering Sea, the Russian acquisition of Alaska in the eighteenth century led immediately to missionary activity in the region. Its first diocese was established at Sitka (then Novoarchangelsk) in 1840, under Saint Innocent of Alaska (Veniaminov) (1797–1879), who later became Metropolitan of Moscow. The seat was transferred to San Francisco in 1872, five years after Russia sold Alaska to the United States. Saint Tikhon (Bellavin), later patriarch of Moscow, became bishop there in 1898, serving Alaska, where he first visited in 1900. He served the diocese until 1907, thus giving Russian Orthodoxy firm roots in the United States. During his episcopate, the Russian Orthodox seat was moved to New York. During the last year of his presence, a Pan-American Council was held there. It was officially called, rather confusingly to our ears, the Greek Catholic Russian Orthodox Church of North America. Many of its members by now were not Russian settlers in Alaska but other immigrants, many from what is today Syria, who originally practiced other versions of the Orthodox faith.

But even as the Orthodox communities within and around the Russian Empire were increasing as never before, a growing disaffection of the intelligentsia from the Church was occurring in the great Russian heartland. This trend began in the time of Peter the Great and grew during the Enlightenment. By the end of the nineteenth century, secular values were triumphing in the highest social circles of Russian society, a situation which would lead to unimaginable calamity in the twentieth.

Chapter 7

Church Reform and Reestablishment of the Patriarchate

Vladimir Soloviev

In the late nineteenth century, some theologians of the Russian Orthodox Church sought accommodation with Western European ecumenical religious and philosophical trends. Vladimir Soloviev (1853-1900) was one such proponent of this rapprochement. He also took great inspiration from the writer Fyodor Dostoyevsky, opposed ecumenicism but himself took inspiration from Soloviev. Indeed, the characters of Alyosha and Ivan Karamazov, in Dostoyevsky's *The Brothers Karamazov* (1879–80)*,* are said to have been based on aspects of Soloviev.

Soloviev was a keen advocate of *sobornost* and encouraged an Orthodox ecumenical approach to Roman Catholicism. Unusually for Russian philosophers and theologians of his time, he was also philo-Semitic and a member of the Society for the Promotion of Culture Among the Jews of Russia. His book *The Russian Ideal* (1888) created a sensation. Perceiving Russia to be under greater threat from the east, by China and Japan, Soloviev felt that it was imperative for the Russian Orthodox Church to join forces with those of Roman Catholicism to combat this "Yellow Peril," a popular term in Europe that expressed the fear perceived by many, that Western civilization, Russia included, was under threat of inundation by Asiatic hordes.

Soloviev believed that this variety of ecumenicism would not only protect Russia from such new assaults from the new "Mongols" of this time, but revive the ancient Byzantine concept of *symphony,* according to which Church and State would work in harmony. While the latter was a concept of the ancient Eastern Orthodox Byzantine Church, with roots in the first half of the first millennium AD, the ideal of a reunion of European Christendom under the Roman pontiff clearly distinguished him from traditional Orthodox theology and principles. On the other hand, Soloviev's focus on *sophia*, a mystical conception of wisdom, was to have considerable influence on Orthodoxy, particularly on such Russian Orthodox clerics as Pavel Florensky and Sergei Bulgakov, in the first half of the twentieth century. His influence can also be seen in the establishment, after his death, of the Philosophical and Religious Society in Honor of Vladimir Soloviev (1905), which functioned until after the Bolshevik Revolution. It was but one of a number of such modest institutions founded in this period, in which a considerable religious flourishing can said to have taken place until overtaken by the atheistic horrors of the Revolution, which were far more devastating than any imagined by Soloviev from the Far East.

Saint John of Kronstadt

Perhaps the greatest spiritual figure of the late imperial period and one largely uncontroversial was Saint John of Kronstadt (1829-1908), a married secular priest of the Church of Saint Andrew, on the fortress island of Kronstadt, protecting St. Petersburg in the Gulf of Finland. The comfort that he rendered to the devoutly Orthodox Tsar Alexander III on his deathbed in 1894 was replicated many times over for countless other members of the Russian elite throughout these final decades of the old order. That said, his principal ministry was to the common people and to this end, following in the footsteps of Saint Theophan the Recluse, he exhorted that the Old Church Slavonic liturgy had to be made understandable to all of the laity, to many of whom he ministered. He wrote in his most famous work, *My Life in Christ*, that "all Orthodox Christians should learn to speak the Slavonic language in order to understand the sweet messages of their Mother Church, who educates Her own children to reach heaven, for eternal life."[41] In this great devotional guide, he also discusses many other aspects of the Christian life, as well as the liturgy and prayer. Fully aware of the minefields being laid by anarchists, nihilists, and the other revolutionaries to destroy Holy Mother

---

[41] Saint John of Kronstadt, *Moia zhizn' vo Khriste* (Moscow, 1999), 766.

Russia as an imperial Orthodox state, he was quick to warn, in the wake of the failed 1905 Revolution:

> Just look at what is happening today in the country: everywhere students and workers are fomenting different types of agitation; party rumors which have the objective to destroy the monarchal order as established by God; in consequence, they assist in the defense of foolish and insolent proclamations, which are in contempt of the authority ordained by God.[42]

Saint John's greatest opprobrium was reserved for the world famous author Lev Tolstoy (1828-1910): "For how long, O Lord, willst Thou sustain Lev Tolstoy, this infamous atheist who disturbs the whole world? When finally will you summon him before your tribunal? O Lord, the earth is weary of tolerating his sacrileges."[43]

For Saint John, both the tsar and his people were culpable:

> The fatherland suffers because of the sins of the tsar and the people, because of the lack of faith and short sightedness of the tsar, through his conniving with disbelief and the sacrilege of Lev Tolstoy and of all the so-called civilized world of ministers, functionaries, officials and the student youth.[44]

Tolstoy's own apostasy would culminate in his novel *Resurrection* (1899), in which the Orthodox liturgy itself is grotesquely characterized. For this and other offenses against the faith, Tolstoy was excommunicated by the Most Holy Synod, in February 1901. Ostracized by the Church but lauded by the liberals and radicals, a few days before his death, in November 1910, Tolstoy endeavored to travel to the Optina Monastery. Was he in search of his final spiritual solace? We shall never know, for he died en route at the Astapovo Railway Station. Perhaps the great Russian Orthodox philosopher of religion, Nikolai Berdiaev (1874-1948), should be given the final word on the subject so far:

---

[42] Idem, *Novye groznye slova, 1906-1907* (Moscow, 1993).
[43] Idem, *Predsmertnyi dnevnik (1908)* (Moscow, 2003), 58.
[44] Ibid., 68.

> Tolstoy is Russian to the bone and could only have been
> born in Orthodox Russia, notwithstanding the fact that he
> betrayed it … The simple people believed in the Orthodox
> way. The Orthodox faith in the mind of the great Tolstoy,
> however, collides unavoidably with his reason.[45]

Berdiaev founded Russian Existentialism, a radical movement at that time, but one with an Orthodox spiritual dimension of great depth. It sought to explore God's abiding presence against an earthly background of misery and angst. Alas, the secularization of the *intelligentsia,* which had held sway for decades amongst the upper and educated classes, now increasingly filtered down to the agricultural and industrial layers of society during these early years of the twentieth century. To combat these trends, as well as to improve the Church's administration by a possible reestablishment of the Patriarchate, a Church Council was convoked, in 1906, to make its preparations. This would only reach fruition in the wake of the February Revolution of 1917 and many of its blessings would lay dormant until the end of the Soviet period which followed.

Nikolai Leskov

Another important figure who focused upon Russian Orthodoxy was the Russian author Nikolai Leskov (1831-1895). Many of his stories focused upon the lives of clergymen and missionaries, in particular those proselytizing in Siberia amongst its indigenous peoples. He himself was the son of a criminal investigator but a number of his paternal relations were clerics. His novel *The Cathedral Clergy* (1872) focuses upon the everyday life of a provincial archpriest, in which the true Christianity of the humble is contrasted with what the author perceived to be the more formalistic and hollow practice of the Church hierarchy. Similarly, *On the Edge of the World* (1875) considers the mission of a bishop to Siberia and is said to be based on the life of an actual missionary; it contrasts the moral nobility of the pagan tribesman with the philistinism of the prelates. Moreover, his Orthodox themes notwithstanding, his writings increasingly

---

[45] N. A. Berdiaev, L. Tolstoi, *O russkoi filosofi* (Sverdlovsk, 1991), pp. 38-39.

show a diverse religious point of view sourced in other religious traditions, which contrasted with traditional Orthodox teaching and values.[46]

Anton Chekhov

The great Russian playwright Anton Chekhov (1860-1904) also, on occasion, devoted himself to themes from Orthodoxy, as in his short tale *A Dreary Story* (1889). Its main character is Professor Nikolai Stepanovich – said to be based on the author's own dying brother – contemplating his approaching death and the meaning of life. As Father Robert M. Aria has put it, "The question that emerges from Stepanovich's introspection is 'who or what is the god of the living man?'" For Chekhov the answer rests in a personal God. The God of the "living man" is Christ, who as incarnate love seeks to draw all to himself in a bond of interpersonal communion based on the new commandment to love one another.[47]

Another of Chekhov's short stories with a religious theme is *The Bishop* (1902). It is said to have been based on the life of Mikhail Gribanovsky, Bishop of Taurida, who died in 1898, but which may also have been, in part, a premonition of Chekhov's own demise from tuberculosis a couple of years later. However, the author had also visited the Davidova Pustyn Monastery of the Resurrection at Novy Byt. This monastery is situated near the author's former country seat of Melkovo (now a museum dedicated to his memory), where he made the acquaintance of the hiermonk Ananias, supposed to have been the model for Father Sisoes in the story.[48] As Father Aria puts it with respect to Chekhov's faith, "his Christianity is that of the sojourner who never ceases to grow in the divine life offered by the immanent and transcendent God."[49]

---

[46] K. A. Lantz, "Leskov's *At the Edge of the World*: The Search for an Image of Christ," *Slavic and East European Journal*, 25: 1 (Spring 1981), pp. 34-43.

[47] Father Robert M. Aria, "Anton Chekhov: Atheist, Agnostic or Struggling Orthodox Christian?," static1.squarespace.com (2009), pp. 4-5.

[48] Ibid., p. 4.

[49] Ibid., p. 7

Orthodox Composers

A plethora of Russian Orthodox composers devoted a considerable part of their *œuvre* to the Orthodox liturgy and spirituality. These included Mikhail Glinka (1804-57), Alexander Borodin (1833-87), Nikolai Rimsky-Korsakov (1844-1908), and Sergei Rachmaninoff (1872-1943), in particular, the latter's Liturgy.

In 1837, Glinka published his *Cherubic Hymn*, a reinterpretation of a liturgical element introduced into ancient Byzantine Cristian liturgy by Emperor Justin II in 573 AD. It is still beloved throughout the Christian world, having become an interdenominational favorite of church choirs everywhere. The following year, Glinka became director of the Imperial Chapel in St. Petersburg. His major opus was devoted to the idea of translating the Book of Job into a musical *cum* literary medium (1869). As Pamela Davidson has put it, "in keeping with Christian tradition, Glinka interpreted the Book of Job as a prophecy of Christ, and saw the account of the patriarch's trials and temptation by Satan as a prefiguration of the Saviour's path through suffering to redemption."[50]

Alexander Borodin, too, was greatly influenced by Orthodoxy, not least in his *Heroic Symphony* (Symphony No. 2, from 1869-76). As an American composer has written, "the opening statement, which begins and ends the first movement (Allegro), is bold and triumphant, clearly influenced by Russian Orthodox chant."[51] Borodin's great but unfinished opera *Prince Igor* (1887) focuses upon the campaign of Orthodox Prince Igor who defeats the pagan Polovtsian tribes who were laying waste to Orthodox Rus in 1185.

Among the greatest of Orthodox composers of this period was Nikolai Rimsky-Korsakov, even if his own relationship to the Church was complicated. His *Great Russian Easter Overture* (Op. 36, 1887-88) is based on liturgical themes and traditional liturgical chants from the *Obikhod* (A collection of traditional polyphonic Russian Orthodox liturgical chants based on an original composition of 1575) inform it. The preface includes verses from the psalms, as well as from the Gospel of

---

[50] Pamela Davidson, "Rewriting the Bible: Fedor Glinka and his Long-Suffering Job," *Slavonic and East European Review*, 95: 4, (2017) pp. 601-624.
[51] Dave Koppil, Symphony No. 2 *Alexander Borodin,* www.laphil.com, 2020.

Saint Mark. As such, it is one of the great musical expressions of Orthodox spirituality of any period, the composer's own self-declared secularism notwithstanding. Furthermore, he wrote music for liturgical use, including a couple of versions of the Cherubic hymn and harmonized an old Russian chant melody for the *irmoi* (verses of each individual ode in a canon) of Holy Saturday.

Sergei Rachmaninoff concluded this great flourishing of Russian Orthodox Music with the major a cappella choral works, *The Liturgy of St John Chrysostom* (op. 31, 1910) and *All-Night Vigil* (Op. 37, 1915). The former, when first performed in Moscow that year, fell afoul of the ecclesiastical authorities because of its modern musical elements. Therefore, it was not accepted at the time as a suitable musical framework for the Russian Orthodox liturgy. That said, it was well received in 1914, in New York City, where the Choir of the Russian Orthodox Church of Saint Nicholas performed it to great acclaim.

Rachmaninoff was especially moved by the *All-Night Vigil* and specified that its *Vespers* should be sung at his funeral. The work evinces the musical elements of chant as traditionally sung in the sixteenth and seventeenth centuries and is today the most popularly cherished musical articulation of the Russian Orthodox liturgy. Another musical composition, which he also desired to have sung at his funeral, was *The Bells* (Op. 35, 1913). This symphony with choral accompaniment drew its inspiration from the unique beauty and spirituality of Orthodox bellringing, especial important at Easter time. However, the words were derived from what might seem a most unlikely source: an eponymous poem by the American poet Edgar Allan Poe, as translated by the Russian Symbolist poet Konstantin Belmont.

The First World War

By 1914, the Russian Empire was enjoying rapid industrial development, a major growth in literacy, and a deep spirituality grounded in Russian Orthodoxy. Indeed, it had an Orthodox population of 98,363,874, out of a total of some 160,000,000 total inhabitants, many of whom were Muslim, Jewish, and Buddhist, as well as Christians of other denominations. These Russian Orthodox were served by some 54,923 churches and 953 monasteries. They, in turn, were staffed by 117,915 clerics and 94,629 monks and nuns.[52] As such, the Russian Empire boasted the largest body of Orthodox faithful in the world, and it formed the empire's predominant religious community.

Hilarion

Some Orthodox theologians were also amongst the greatest thinkers of the time. The Russian hermit Hilarion (died 1916) formulated the doctrine of the divine nature of the name of God and Jesus, in his book *On the Mountains of the Caucasus* (1907). This work stresses the importance of the Jesus Prayer, discussed in Chapter 6. This focus was supported by the great Russian Orthodox theologians Fathers Sergei Bulgakov (1851-1917), Pavel Florensky (1882-1937), and Nikolai Berdiaev (1874-1948). However, Hilarion's doctrine incurred the wrath of powerful members of the Holy Synod, in particular, Archbishop Antonii Khrapovitsky (1863-1936). Nonetheless, there were many in the monastic world who shared Hilarion's views – including no less than a thousand Russian monks at the Saint Panteleimon Monastery on Mount Athos. In consequence, in 1903, they were expelled and, in 1913, the Most Holy Synod officially condemned this doctrine. Even so, it is debated to this day.

Nikolai Berdiaev

One of Hilarion's supporters, Nikolai Berdiaev would go on to become one of the most important Russian Orthodox theologians of the twentieth century. As he pointed out, for all the atheism, anarchism, and nihilism of the nineteenth century, Russia's literature remained the most spiritually deep and Christian produced anywhere:

> All of our literature of the nineteenth century is marked by the wounds of Christian themes, and all the reaching out to find salvation, liberation from evil, from suffering, from the horror which life represents for the humanist individual, for the people, for humanity, for the world. In

---

[52] V. Tsypin, "Russkaia pravoslavnaia Tserkov' v sinodal'nuiu epokhu, 1700-1917," *Pravoslavnaia Entsiklopediia*, p.132.

their most significant works they are permeated by religious thought.[53]

For Berdiaev, Orthodoxy was no legalistic religion, but one which was lived and experienced to the core of one's being. "Orthodoxy is not first of all a doctrine or an exterior organization, an external norm extraneous to comportment, but a spiritual life, a spiritual experience and a spiritual road."[54] In this sense, in his view, it stood in contrast to the Roman Catholic spiritual tradition for: "Rationalism, legalism and every type of the normative are alien to Orthodoxy. The Orthodox Church is not defined by rational conceits; rather it is only comprehensible to those who participate in the experience of its spirituality."[55]

Individualism is not the key element, but subsumed within the whole community, which enjoys the freedom that Orthodoxy conveys. Thus, the most important liturgical event of the year is Easter, that is, the celebration of Christ's Resurrection, which brought freedom from death to all true believers. None of these beliefs, however, led Berdiaev to reject the rich spiritual values of the Western churches. He was thus an ecumenical figure: "The recognition of the exceptional spiritual values of Orthodoxy, as the purest form of Christianity, should not create in it a self-complacency and lead to a negation of the values of Western Christianity. On the contrary we should acquaint ourselves with the Western church and learn much from it. We should strive for Christian unity."[56]

Saint Maksim Sandovich

The First World War paved the wave for the catastrophe which swept away not only the Russian, German, Austro-Hungarian, and Ottoman Empires, but also shook the very foundations of European society. A firm adherence to the Orthodox faith was seen by Imperial Germany and Austria-Hungary less as a personal religious choice than as loyalty to the enemy, for whom it was the established religion. For this reason, Saint

---

[53] N. A. Berdiaev, "O kharaktere russkoi religioznoi mysli XIX veka," *O russkoi filosofi* (Sverdlovsk 1991), II, p. 23.
[54] Idem, "Istina Pravoslaviia," *Vestnik Russkogo Zapadno-Evropeiskogo Patriarshego Ekzarkhata* (Paris, 1952) p. 5.
[55] Ibid., 5.
[56] Ibid., 10

Maksim Sandovich (1888-1914), born into the Lemko ethnic community of Transcarpathia, was among the war's first Orthodox hieromartyrs. He was executed as a Russian spy at Gorlice, now in Poland, in early August 1914. His martyrdom became a rallying point for growing Orthodox hostility to the Habsburg regime, which sought to impose Roman Catholicism on the Orthodox population after its occupation.

Revolution and the Convocation of the Council of 1917

Unquestionably, though, the greatest assault on Orthodox religious belief in the Russian Empire was carried out not by those governments at war with it but by Russian citizens themselves. Many of them desired the overthrow and destruction of the imperial system and those who supported it. Some of the most ardent revolutionaries were among the clergy themselves. In March, in the wake of the February Revolution, Prince Georgy Lvov, then Prime Minister, was deeply concerned that anti-war bishops would undermine the war effort and secured their removal from office.

Others, however, supported the legitimate imperial authorities. Hieromartyr Saint and Bishop Andrei (Ukhtomsky, 1872-1937) of Ufa exhorted a large crowd assembled in front of Kazan Cathedral in Petrograd, as St. Petersburg was renamed, to "esteem your officers, be submissive to them, and the enemy at the front will be broken."[57] When this failed to placate the mobs, the Most Holy Synod issued two obligatory sermons, in which both the war dead and those who had died during the February Revolution were commemorated. This dovetailed with the desires of the liberal All-Russian Congress of Democratic Clergy and Laymen, which had supported the revolution but remained committed to victory in the war against Germany. A *Te Deum* was sung in Red Square in Moscow and a Victory Procession was held in front of Saint Isaac's Cathedral, in Petrograd, in early June, under the false belief that such success was at hand.[58] In August 1917 a Church Council was convened –

---

[57] Adrian Gregory, "Beliefs and Religion," in *Cambridge History of the First World War, Volume III: Civil Society*, Jay Winter, ed. (Cambridge, 2014), p. 425
[58] Ibid., pp. 425-426.

the largest ever held in Russia. Its work continued during and after the Bolshevik Revolution, into 1918. This was the first such council to be held since the pre-Petrine times. Most importantly, in November 1917 the Patriarchate was reestablished and Tikhon (Bellavin), Metropolitan of Moscow (1865-1925), who had formerly led the Russian Orthodox Church in the United States, was chosen as the first Patriarch in over two centuries, a bright candle of hope against an otherwise backdrop of misery and despair.

Independence of the Georgian Orthodox Church

A deleterious effect of the Revolution of 1917 was the dissolution of the administrative unity of the Russian Orthodox Church, which has continued into our own day. In 1917, the Russian Orthodox Church commanded great spiritual authority in Georgia. With no fewer than 2,455 churches serving its faithful, its hierarchy was in a position of great strength at that time. However, with feelings of Georgian nationalism rising, and the increasing threat of the Bolsheviks assuming control of the apparatus of the state, it declared its independence from the Moscow Patriarchy. Its local synod then elected a catholicos-patriarch as its spiritual and administrative head, an act condemned by the Russian Orthodox Church, which, in consequence, broke off communion with it. This would set an unfortunate precedent throughout the newly established or reestablished states of the former Russian Empire, which presaged the schism in Ukraine today. Yet the assault on the Church, from both within and without, was not only administrative. Ultimately, it struck at the heart of its spirituality and mission: within only a few years, thousands of clergy and millions of faithful would be its victims.

Saint Seraphin of Vyritsa

Even in the early dark days of the incipient Soviet state, Orthodox spirituality and steadfastness could prevail. One of the most spiritually prominent martyrs during the early Soviet period was the Venerable Saint Seraphin of Viritsa (Basil Muraviev, 1865-1949). He had become a monk later in life, his marriage and three children notwithstanding, entering the Saint Alexander Nevsky Lavra, in what was by then Leningrad, in 1927. He fell afoul of the atheistic regime and was imprisoned from 1927 until

1933, in the gulag network of Soviet labor camps. Upon his release, he settled at Viritsa, a small town south of Leningrad where he served in a small wooden church dedicated to the Kazan Icon of the Most Holy Theotokos (Mother of God). The church had only recently been built to commemorate the tricentenary of the Romanov dynasty, in 1913. There he became a *starets* noted for his great spirituality and wise spiritual and practical advice. One of his most famous adages was prescient for our own times:

> There will come a time when not the persecutions, but money and the goods of this world will take people far from God. Then many more souls will be lost than in the time of the persecutions. On the one hand, they will be putting gold on the domes and will put the crosses on them and, on the other hand, everywhere evil and falsehood will reign. The true Church will always be persecuted. They who want to be saved will be saved with illnesses and afflictions.[59]

---

[59] Quoted by Mother Maria Yakovleva of the Saint Elisabeth Convent, Kiev, 21 March 2020

Chapter 8

Soviet Persecution

The Persecution of the Church Commences

Despite the reestablishment of the patriarchate, the road to cavalry which the Russian Orthodox Church itself in countless ways was to endure during the Soviet period came as no surprise. After all, Vladimir Lenin, the Soviet leader, was a militant atheist. Already in 1905, he had published his notorious views on the Church in the article "Socialism and Religion," in which he exclaimed, following Karl Marx, that "Religion is the opium of the people."[60] In consequence, he was determined to extinguish it by any means, however violent, as if it were a drug addiction undermining the whole of society.

The Bolshevik Revolution, an event which would undermine not only Russia itself but the Russian Church in countless ways, broke out on 25 October 2017 (old calendar). The next day, 26 October, a decree of the Supreme Soviet nationalized all church and monastic property, along with any ancillary wealth. The Soviets then turned their attention to the clergy. Five days later, Father John Kochurov (1871-1917) became the first of thousands of clergymen to be martyred. On 22 January 1918, the Russian Orthodox Church was formally disestablished. The Soviet government decreed separation of Church and State and banned religious education. A few days later of Metropolitan Vladimir (Bogoyavlensky) of Kiev, an outspoken critic of these outrages, was murdered. Patriarch Tikhon anathematized the Bolsheviks, but his exhortations fell on deaf ears and the slaughter continued to claim not only countless other prelates and clerics of the Church but the Imperial Family itself. Stoically bearing their incarceration and ultimate martyrdom, in Ekaterinburg, just east of the

---

[60] V. I. Lenin, *Polnoe sobranie sochinenii,* Vol. 12 (Moscow, 1979), p.143.

Ural Mountains, they were eventually canonized, embodying Christian stoicism in the face of persecution.

Patriarch Tikhon's Attempts to Preserve Church Integrity

As Patriarch Tikhon exclaimed from the pulpit of the Cathedral of Our Lady of Kazan:

> In these days, a horrendous crime has been committed: the former sovereign Nicholas Alexandrovich has been shot and our supreme authority, our government, the executive committee, has approved and recognized this action has legitimate … However, our Christian conscience, informed by the words of God, cannot accept something of this type. We must, obeying the teachings of the words of God, condemn this action. Otherwise the blood of those shot will fall upon us, and not only on those who have committed this act.[61]

Heedless of his words, the massacres of broad swathes of the population not only continued but accelerated. On 26 October 1918, the Patriarch expounded to the Soviet authorities in a published letter:

> You have divided the people into two inimical camps and plunged them into a fratricidal war of such cruelty as has never been seen experienced before. You have substituted the love of Christ with hatred and brought about such a peace as is artificially fed by class warfare … No one is safe and everyone lives in a state of constant terror of searches, sackings, expulsions, arrests and executions.[62]

Patriarch Tikhon soon found himself under house arrest and was obliged to witness, from February 1919, that many saintly relics of Church were being desecrated in a systematic way. Some of those preserved were transferred to the Cathedral of Our Lady of Kazan, which had been turned into the Museum of Atheism. Others were transferred to existing museums.

---

[61] M. Polskii, *Novye mucheniki rossiiskie* (Jordanville, NY: 1957), Vol. 1, pp. 282–283.
[62] Alfeev, *La chiesa ortodossa*, p. 279.

With Russia in the midst of civil war and plagued by famine, the Bolshevik authorities considered it expedient to use Patriarch Tikhon as the titular head of a commission to attract charitable funds from abroad. The renowned author Maksim Gorky served as the intermediary between the Church and the Soviet state. The state authorities were not content with the contributions from the wider Christian churches abroad, however. From December 1921, they obliged the Russian Orthodox Church to relinquish all of its valuable non-liturgical treasures, amassed over the preceding centuries. In February 1922, even liturgical vessels were included in this sacrilege.

Popular resistance to these measures, as at Shuya, in Ivanovo Province, was rapidly crushed by the Red Army with merciless brutality. Lenin stood at the vanguard of this movement and saw the occasion of the famine as the perfect opportunity to devastate the Church. The brutal conclusion took place on 30 March 1922: the Patriarch and members of the Holy Synod were all arrested. Metropolitan Benjamin (Kazansky) of Petrograd, together with another eighty-five other clerics, was brought to trial for opposing the regime's will. Condemned to death with several others, the Metropolitan was executed by firing squad. By then, about half the prelates of the Church had fled abroad, necessitating the consecration of other clerics to fill, if only partially, the void left behind.

Internal disputes within the Church also broke out. Some clerics sought accommodation with the new regime and with the growing secularity of the age. Some supported such innovations as clerical marriages after ordination, which broke with ancient cannon law, as well as a revocation of the excommunication of the late Lev Tolstoy. Sensing an opportunity to create divisions in the Church that would serve their purpose of undermining it, the Soviet state supported those who opposed Patriarch Tikhon and his adherence to strict canon law. Those in opposition to Tikhon at first included only the archbishops of Vladimir, Nizhnii Novgorod, and Kostroma, but they were soon joined by many other high clerics, with only thirty-six remaining faithful to tradition. In consequence, a pseudo-council was convoked, with 476 ecclesiastical delegates participating. Patriarch Tikhon refused to accept their decisions but in early 1923 he was taken to the notorious Lubyanka Prison, in

Moscow, for interrogation by the secret police. There they attempted to force him to recant his "anti-Soviet" activity. He was eventually released and published the following:

> I have never proclaimed, certainly, support for the Soviet regime which supports the innovators of the Church … but at same time I am no enemy as it portrays me … I condemn in the briefest of terms every attack on the Soviet regime, from whichever side it may come. Monarchists and the supporters of the Whites, both within and outside of the country, now know for certain that I am not an enemy of the Soviet regime.[63]

By the end of August 1923, the innovators had largely recanted and a certain unity was restored thanks to St Tikhon's conciliatory approach to the regime.

The following year, however, there was a resurgence of those who sought to implement the innovations just rejected, but, this time, with the support of the Ecumenical Patriarch of Constantinople, Gregory VII. This was only another example of the occasions through the centuries in which the Orthodox leader stood in opposition to his Muscovite counterpart. Gregory exhorted Patriarch Tikhon to resign and for the Patriarchate to be put in at least temporary abeyance, all of which moves were rejected by Tikhon.

The unity of the Russian Orthodox Church was also threatened from another direction: namely, from clerics who had emigrated abroad in flight from the Soviet regime. Many of them assembled at a council in Constantinople, held in 1920, and established an ecclesiastical administration there, under the authority of Anthony (Khrapovitsky) (1863-1936), Metropolitan of Kiev and Galicia. Their goal was not to undermine church unity but to constitute a church authority that could legitimately minister to the millions of Russian émigrés now abroad.

A new pseudo-council held in Moscow, in the spring of 1923, dominated by the so-called innovators, deposed Tikhon, a decision he refused to accept. Gregory responded by suspending communion between the two major branches of Orthodoxy. Tikhon issued an *ukaz* which

---

[63] Saint Tikhon, *Akty Sviataishego Tikhona* (Moscow), p. 283.

allowed for an independent administration of local bishops until such time as normal communications with Moscow could be restored.

The following year this administration moved to Sremskie Karlovcy, in what had become Yugoslavia. Under Soviet pressure, Tikhon made some attempts to suppress this new synod in exile, but they were unsuccessful and it continued to function. In 1924, the beleaguered Patriarch escaped an assassination attempt that killed his secretary. Soon after, his health radically declined.

As death approached, the Soviet authorities attempted to force Tikhon to write a letter of support for them, while condemning the synod in exile. He refused to collaborate and died shortly thereafter. Nonetheless, the letter was published with what is now said to be a falsified signature. Nonetheless, it had little effect. The Russian Orthodox Church Outside Russia (ROCOR) now split from Moscow, while more and more priests within the Soviet Union were persecuted by the Soviet regime. The separated churches only reconciled in 2007.

By 1926, some twenty bishops who had remained in the Soviet Union had been incarcerated in the ancient Solovetsky Monastery, situated on an island in the White Sea, just below the Arctic Circle in the far north. With political pressure mounting, in 1927 (and then again in 1934), the acting church authorities, especially Metropolitan Sergei (Stragorodsky), were obliged to issue condemnations of the synod of the Russia Orthodox Church Abroad, in an infamous *Declaration*, which also functionally signaled the capitulation of the Church to the Soviet authorities on all fronts. In 1927, with matters thus reaching a head and in reaction to his declaration, the synod abroad finally officially broke away from Moscow, or at least from Sergei. In their liturgical commemorations, they continued to pray for Tikhon's legitimate successor, *locus tenens* Metropolitan Peter of Krutitsa, until news of his death in 1937 – he was shot in the Russian Arctic, by order of the secret police.

It was the church in exile that started to thrive abroad, while the Russian Orthodox Church, in the Soviet Union itself, withered away under a persecution of dimensions unknown even in the worst days of the Mongol yoke seven hundred years before. In 1928, 354 churches were closed and, in 1929, 1,119, of which at least 322 were destroyed. In 1930,

Moscow suffered the worst depredations, with 276 churches destroyed out of the city's total of about 500.[64] This onslaught culminated in the destruction in 1931 of the Cathedral of Christ the Savior. Dreadful as this was, the destruction of churches was increasingly supplemented by the deportations, incarcerations, and executions of clerics, as advocated by the state-supported Society of Militant Atheists. Both clerics who followed traditional cannon law and those who had sought innovations under Soviet pressure now found themselves targets of an anti-clerical oppression which knew no limits. Indeed, in 1935, the synod of the innovators was also completely suppressed.

By the eve of the Second World War, only about one hundred churches remained open, and all monasteries and religious institutes had ceased to function in their spiritual mission. In Ukraine, the situation was even worse, with only three per cent of existing churches still open. Moreover, only a fraction of the episcopal administration of the Church still continued their clerical duties: Sergei, Metropolitan of Moscow; Aleksei (Simansky), Metropolitan of Leningrad; Nikolai (Yarushevich), Archbishop of Peterhof, ordinary of Novgorod and Pskov; and Sergei (Voskresensky), Archbishop of Dimitrov were still permitted to carry on their ministry, but under enormous constraints. The Dormition Monastery of the Caves, near Pskov, during the interwar years in Estonia, and carried on unimpeded, unlike all the monasteries of the Soviet Union itself where almost all suffered massive devastation. When the Dormition was reincorporated into the Soviet Union, in 1944, the worst period of desecration was over and it has remained intact into our own day, albeit used towards the end of the war and thereafter as a camp for political prisoners, many of them monks and priests.

In Poland, too, the Russian Orthodox Church suffered, as fierce Catholic nationalists carried out the demolition of Warsaw's nineteenth-century Russian Orthodox Cathedral of Alexander Nevsky. A further 120 Russian Orthodox churches were also destroyed in Chołm and Podlasi, with thousands of Orthodox faithful coerced into converting to Roman Catholicism.[65]

---

[64] Alfeev, *La Chiesa Ortodossa*, pp. 289–290.
[65] Ibid., 333

The Second World War and Church Revival

With the conclusion of the Molotov-Ribbentrop Pact, prior to the outbreak of World War II in 1939, eastern areas of Poland were annexed by the Soviet Union. In 1940, the USSR annexed the old Russian province of Bessarabia from Romania, as well as Northern Bukovina. The Soviets also seized the Baltic states of Latvia, Lithuania, and Estonia. This not only increased the Orthodox population of the Soviet Union but meant that no fewer than 3,021 functioning churches and 88 monasteries came under Soviet hegemony.[66]

The storm against the Church eventually abated. With the unexpected Nazi German assault on the Soviet Union in June 1941, all resources were mobilized to stir up the population on behalf of Mother Russia. From 1943, a certain tolerance for Russian Orthodoxy became the order of the day, since most Orthodox faithful could be expected to come to the aid of their country, even in its Soviet guise. Metropolitan Sergei exhorted the faithful to come to the aid of the Soviet Union, proclaiming:

> The Fascist scoundrels have attacked our fatherland. Breaking every accord and promise they made with us, they have suddenly attacked us, and the blood of our peaceful citizens now flows on our soil. The times have returned of Batu, the German knights, of Charles of Sweden, of Napoleon ... But it is not for the first time that the Russian people are obliged to withstand a test of this kind. With the help of God, they will reduce the fascist foe to dust.[67]

In September 1943, Stalin invited Metropolitans Sergei (Stragorodsky), Alexei (Simansky) and Nikolai (Yarushevich) to a personal meeting to organize an election of both a new patriarch and synod.[68] A few days later Metropolitan Sergei was duly elected and enthroned as patriarch. However, he died the following year, to be succeed by Alexei (Simansky). Stalin and the Soviet regime were now giving the Russian Orthodox

---

[66] Ibid., 292-293.

[67] *Russkaia Pravoslavnaia tserkov' i velikaia otechestvennaia voina. Sbornik dokumentov* (Moscow 1943), pp. 3-5.

[68] Alfeev, *La Chiesa Ortodossa*, pp. 293-94.

Church the juridical right to exist. Many Orthodox faithful were unconvinced and the Germans, realizing the importance of Orthodoxy to large swathes of the Soviet population, encouraged its revival in the occupied territories. Perhaps it was this rather than fostering defense of the motherland that led Stalin to permit the legitimacy of the Church.

Abrogation of the Union of Brest

The end of the Second World War at first boded well for a revival of the Russian Orthodox Church. With the redrawing of borders that favored the victorious Soviet Union, and the accession of Patriarch Alexei, more than three thousand Greek Catholic parishes were absorbed into the Russian Orthodox fold. While Stalin did this for reasons of state, rather than for spiritual reasons, the church rejoiced. Many of its clergy and laity now felt that an injustice introduced by the Polish-Lithuanian Commonwealth by the Union of Brest had been corrected. Two years later, the Russian Patriarchate granted a status of autocephaly to the Polish Orthodox Church. The Church enjoyed a significant revival in these conditions. By early 1949, there were some 73 clergymen of episcopal standing, 75 functioning monasteries, two theological academies, eight seminaries, and no fewer than 14,477 functioning churches.[69] However, many of these were in newly conquered Soviet territories where, during the interwar years, they had remained open. In any case, this revival would prove to be short lived.

Khrushchev and Renewed Persecution of the Church

After the death of Stalin, in March 1953, many Orthodox prisoners of conscience were liberated. However, from 1958, under Premier Nikita Khrushchev, a virulent atheist period of renewed persecution began. Some 1,234 people were imprisoned on religious grounds. Churches, monasteries, and seminaries were closed again. By 1966, only 7,523 churches were functioning in the Soviet Union.[70]

---

[69] Ibid., p. 295.
[70] Ieromonach Damaskin (Orlovskii) "Goneniia na Russkuiu Tserkov,'' *Pravoslavnaia entsiklopediia* (Moscow), p. 188.

Scientific Atheism was again becoming the order of the day, with all manner of pressure used by the regime to suppress religious belief and practice. On occasion even priests, sometimes secretly alienated from the Church for personal reasons, served the KGB as moles from within to spy on other priests. [71] Moreover, faithful bishops were often obliged to collaborate with the regime to weed out those hostile to the Soviet system, especially candidates for clerical positions.

Nikodim, Metropolitan of Leningrad

Not all was doom and gloom, however. During the 1960s, Metropolitan Nikodim (Rotov) of Leningrad assumed a leading role in the Church. He opened seminaries to foreign students and encouraged a limited degree of ecumenicism, in particular with the Roman Catholic Church, although he was criticized for that by more conservative clerical figures. He was widely said to have been involved in negotiating an agreement between the Vatican and Soviet Union, enabling Russian Orthodox participation in the Second Vatican Council of 1962-1965. He attended in person and died in the Vatican during the installation of Pope John Paul I in 1978, prayed over by the new pontiff, who was himself to die just over a month later. One conspiracy theory has suggested that Nikodim had drunk a poisoned cup of tea meant for the pope himself!

The wider Russian Orthodox Church remained in a period of stagnation. By 1988, the number of parishes had shrunk to 6,893 in the whole of the Soviet Union. [72] Who could have anticipated at this time the massive resurrection of Russian Orthodoxy that followed after the fall of the Soviet Union, with millions of faithful rushing to its churches, a trend which has continued until now?

Father Alexander Men

Perhaps the swan song of Russian Orthodoxy during the final years of the Soviet Union was sung by an unusual priest, Father Alexander Men (1935-90), who was murdered on his way to church during the final year of Soviet

---

[71] S. L. Firsov, *Apostasiia. "Ateist Aleksandr Osipov i epokha khrushchevskikh gonenii na Russkuiu Pravoslavnuiu Tserkov* (St. Petersburg, 2004), pp. 197 and 231.
[72] Alfeev, *La Chiesa Ortodossa*, p. 298.

rule. His murder was never solved, but many consider him a martyr to his faith because of the many enemies he made, some even within his own family. Born of Jewish parents who were said to have converted to "catacomb" Orthodoxy, a non-canonical offshoot about which it is difficult to separate truth from fiction, and which was said to have refused collaboration with both the Soviet Moscow Patriarchate and the Russian Orthodox Church Abroad.

Be that as it may, the Men family did secretly convert to Orthodoxy. Their son's approach to his Orthodox faith had eclectic sources, including some from non-Christian religions. It also gave birth in his spirit to a powerful ecumenism. This earned him many enemies in conservative church circles who felt that Orthodoxy should not accommodate Roman Catholic or any other body of religious dogma and practice. With a background at the Moscow Theological Academy, Men was a prolific writer whose most famous books include *Son of Man* (published under a pseudonym in 1969) and his six volume *History of Religion*, published in Brussels in the 1970s and 1980s and finally in Moscow in 1991. He was perhaps most appreciated abroad, especially in Great Britain, where Metropolitan Anthony of Surozh, a deeply revered cleric of respected Russian Orthodox credentials, greatly admired him and where his influence can still be felt today.

Chapter 9

The Diaspora of
the Russian Orthodox Church

The principal church organization of the diaspora which developed outside the Soviet Union was the Russian Orthodox Church Outside Russia (ROCOR). In November 1920, Saint Tikhon, Patriarch of Moscow, together with the Most Holy Synod, informed the bishops of the Church, many of whom had gone into exile, that they might organize and administer themselves, should links to Moscow be severed. In consequence, a new ecclesiastical administration was set up, under the leadership of Antony (Khrapovitsky) (1863-1936), Metropolitan of Kiev and Galicia, in the presence of the martyred tsar's cousin Grand Duke Alexander Mikhailovich. Permission to do this was granted not by the Patriarch or Synod in Moscow, but by the Ecumenical Patriarch in Constantinople, who before the First World War had given permission to Russian bishops to minister to the needs of Orthodox Ottoman subjects, through his *locum tenens* or representative Orthodox Metropolitan Dorotheus of Prussia. They were now ministering to the faithful on neither Russian nor former Ottoman territory but in exile, so his permission no longer mattered. Several years later, among some of those who remained under Moscow's leadership, it was called the Schism of Karlovci, a city located in the newly formed state of Yugoslavia. Many of the faithful who came within its fold were former members of General Wrangel's White Army, which had previously taken an active role in the Russian Civil War.[73]

---

[73] Irina du Quenoy, "An Unlikely Reconciliation: The Path of the Russian Orthodox Church Outside of Russia toward Canonical Union with the Moscow Patriarchate," *Acta Slavica Iaponica*, 2021.

In 1922, the Synod of the Ecumenical Orthodox Church unilaterally decreed that all the Orthodox churches of the Russian diaspora should be henceforth placed under its jurisdiction. This was already the case with the autonomous monastic state of Mount Athos, with its numerous of Orthodox monasteries of different ethnicities, including the Russian Orthodox Monastery of Saint Panteleimon, which in the early twentieth century provided more than half of the monks present on Mount Athos, that is, some 1,500 monks.[74] Most Orthodox Churches with their own national administrative autonomy refused to accept this decision. In eastern Czechoslovakia, today's Slovakia but then carved out of the former Austrian-Hungarian Empire, the Orthodox Church continued to find its faithful among the ethnic Ukrainians who administered it. In 1920, it became autocephalous but from 1924 some of its parishes came under Serbian jurisdiction while others remained within the Russian Orthodox Church Outside Russia. In 1946, after the Soviet takeover, they were reunited with that of Moscow. However, in 1951, it became autocephalous again.

The Finnish Orthodox Church, formerly under Moscow, became autonomous in 1923 and came under the jurisdiction of the Ecumenical Patriarch. Its primate is the Bishop of Helsinki and all Finland. The New Valamo (Valaam) Monastery, was transferred from the great Monastery of Valaam, on an island in Lake Ladoga, in formerly Finnish Karelia, after the Winter War. The Lintula Convent of the Holy Trinity, founded in 1895, on the isthmus of what had formerly been Finnish Karelia, opposite the island on which Valaam was located, moved to Heinävesi, in Finland, in 1946. (It should be noted that in the post-Soviet period, the old Valaam Monastery, on Lake Ladoga, has reopened its doors and blossomed, welcoming clerics, laity and leaders of Russia, some of whom, including President Putin, have a domicile and private chapel on the island.)

In the United States, in the 1920s, the Russian Orthodox Church Abroad became a multi-ethnic church, with clerics and faithful from a wide range of Orthodox ethnicities. This followed in a tradition already established by Saint Tikhon, later Patriarch of Moscow, when he was bishop there in the early years of the twentieth century. In the wake of the

---

[74] Alfeev, *La Chiesa Ortodossa*, p. 322.

Revolution, the American parishes continued to exist as a separate Metropolia, which initially recognized the authority of the Church Abroad, but then removed, reinstated, and then removed it again – a confused state of affairs.

After the Second World War, the leadership of the Russian Orthodox Church Abroad, which had been based in Europe, moved to the United States. Effectively then, in 1948, two separate ecclesiastical jurisdictions had come to be firmly established, the Russian Orthodox Church Outside Russia and the Metropolia. This eventually became the Orthodox Church of America, its autocephaly granted by the Russian Orthodox Church in Moscow. However, the Ecumenical Patriarch has refused it recognition to this day. For all their distinctness, however, each sees itself as the spiritual descendant of both Saint Herman of Alaska and Saint Tikhon, much as the Russian Orthodox Church and autonomous Ukrainian Orthodox Church do to this day, with respect to the holy fathers of over a millennium ago in Kiev. Father Alexander Schmeman and Saint Vladimir's Seminary went with the Metropolia/Orthodox Church of America, while the Russian Orthodox Church outside Russia had its own seminary, the Holy Trinity Monastery, at Jordanville, New York. Serbian, Romanian, and Bulgarian Orthodox Churches also eventually came into being, each more or less autonomous and out of communion with the mother churches in Europe after the Iron Curtain fell over their countries, stifling Orthodox spiritual life at home. In consequence, by the 1950s, Saint Vladimir's Seminary, with its roots in that of Saint-Serge in Paris, had become a multi-Orthodox establishment for a wide range of ethnic Orthodox churches. Founded in 1938, in Yonkers, a suburb of New York City, it attracted figures of the Theological School of Paris who pulled up stakes and moved to the United States there, including Shmeman, Georges Florovsky and John Meyendorff. They became deans at the seminary, which by then had become an important center of Russian Orthodox study in the United States, competing with the Holy Trinity Monastery at Jordanville and Saint Tikhon's Seminary, also of the Orthodox Church of America, in South Canaan, Pennsylvania.

Saint Vladimir's Seminary was eventually accredited with the State University of New York, and had its own English-language printing press. Yet it was Jordaneville's printing press, which traced its roots to the Pochaev Monastery in Ukraine, that became world renowned in Orthodox circles, not least because of its Russian-language books that it smuggled into the Soviet Union, where theological study and publications languished under the shackles of atheistic rulers. This strengthened rifts within the wider Orthodox world so that while Russian and other branches of Orthodoxy increasingly thrived in America, only in the mid 1990s did dialogue recommence between the Russian Orthodox Patriarchate of Moscow and the Ecumenical Patriarch of Constantinople, the latter having come to see himself as the titular head of world Orthodoxy.

Sergei Bulgakov

Sergei Bulgakov (1871-1944) was one of the most important theologians of the interwar period. His life was dedicated to creating a comprehensive systematization of Orthodoxy, drawing on its traditions, cannon laws, teachings of the fathers, liturgy and collected doctrines. As he wrote:

> Tradition is the living memory of the Church, which contains the true doctrine as it is revealed in its history. It is not an archaeological museum or a scientific catalogue, nor is it a dead 'deposit' of the faith: it is a living force, in a living organization. In the flux of its own life, tradition carries with it all of the parts in all of its components and in all times.[75]

For the hierarchy of both the Moscow Patriarchate and the Russian Church Outside Russia, however, the concept on which this is based, namely that of the Sofiology, as set out by Solovyev and Florensky, was anathema. Therefore, both Metropolitan Sergei of Moscow and the Synod of the Russian Church Abroad condemned it. Nevertheless, many of his ideas continued to influence Orthodox theologians, especially in the Diaspora.

The role of Metropolitan Euolgius (Georgievsky, 1868-1946) should also be mentioned here because of the divisions that led to the establishment of the Parisian jurisdiction under the Patriarchate of Constantinople, which split from the Russian Orthodox Church Outside

---

[75] S. Bulgakov *Pravoslavie. Ocherki ucheniia Pravoslavnoi Tserkvi* (Paris, 1989), pp.47–48.

Russia and eventually returned to the Moscow Patriarchate. The Institute of Saint Sergei was a part of this jurisdiction, even though some of its leading figures, like Archimandrite Cyprian Kern, went back and forth.

The Orthodox Theological Institute of Paris

The Saint Sergei Theological Institute of Paris rapidly became the center of Orthodox studies in Europe during the interwar years. It was founded in 1925 to educate Orthodox priests and laymen, and was established in a building originally built for use as a German Lutheran church. Theologically, it was characterized by four schools of thought, all with an emphasis on ecumenicism. Among the most famous figures of the first school, in theological terms, was Father Georges Florovsky (1893—1979), a native of Odessa. He focused on Russian Orthodox patristic studies and published his influential theological work, *Eastern Fathers of the Fourth Century,* in 1931. This was followed by *The Byzantine Fathers. Fifth to Eight Centuries,* in 1933, and his magisterial work, *The Ways of Russian Theology,* in 1937. All of these works turned away from the contemporary theological focus on the scholastic and pietistic theological traditions of the second millennium. This new focus had its roots in both Catholic and Protestant Western European thought, but unlike those of other Christian traditions Florovsky sought a return to the earlier Byzantine theological roots of the Orthodox Church. This approach nonetheless earned him the opprobrium of some of his contemporary Orthodox theologians, in particular, Nikolai Berdyaev.

Father Vladimir Lossky (1903-58), born of a Russian father in Göttingen, Germany, played an equally important role in Paris at this time. He would go on to become first dean of the Saint Dionysius Orthodox Institute in Paris, established in 1944, which, its Russian roots notwithstanding, attracted Roman Catholics as well Orthodox believers. Lossky, too, drew his theological inspiration from the early centuries of the Church in Byzantium. His most famous work, *The Mystical Theology of the Eastern Church* (1944), focuses upon its apophatic character. This theological approach seeks to understand God less in defining his positive attributes but rather in clarifying the characteristics which cannot be applied to Him, thereby giving an intense focus on His mystical aspects.

Other important theological figures of this tradition included Archbishop Vasily (Krivoshein, 1900-85), Archimandrite Cyprian (Kern, 1909-60), and Father John von Meyendorff (1926-92).

The second school of thought focused on liturgical issues. Nikolai Afanasyev (1893-1966) and Alexander Shmeman (1921-83) were among its chief figures.

The third school was preoccupied with historical and cultural matters. Its most noted figures were Sergei Chetverikov (1867-1947), Anton Kartashev (1875-1960), Georgy Fedotov (1886-1951), Konstantin Mochulysky (1892-1948), Ivan Kontsevich (1893-65) and Nicholas Zernov (1898–1980). The latter's introduction to Russian Orthodoxy, *The Russians and Their Church*, was first published in 1945, but enjoyed later reprints.

The fourth school, in turn, was highly philosophical. It included such luminaries as Nikolai Berdyaev, Nikolai Lossky (1870-1965), Boris Vysheslavtsev (1877-1954), Lev Karsavin (1882-1952), Ivan Ilyin (1882-1954), and Vasily Zenkovsky (1881-1962).

Saint John the Baptist Monastery, Essex

Other centers of Russian Orthodox studies which derived from the Theological School of Paris were also established. One such in England is the Monastery of Saint John the Baptist, in the village of Tolleshunt Knights, near Maldon, in Essex (now under the Ecumenical Patriarch's authority but then under the Moscow Patriarchate). It was established in 1959 by the Russian ascetic Saint Sophrony (Sakharov, 1896-1993), who became an archimandrite there. Devout from childhood, Sophrony had first studied art at the Russian Imperial Academy of Art in St. Petersburg, before emigrating to Paris after the Revolution, and thence to the Russian Monastery of Saint Panteleimon, on Mount Athos. There he was ordained a priest, in 1941. After the Second World War, he moved first to Paris before finally settling in Essex, which rapidly became one of the most important centers of spiritual life in England. There he focused on reviving the spirituality of the fifteenth century Saint Simeon the New Theologian, based on the contemplation of "divine light." This is a mystical concept which focuses on the spiritual communion of the heavenly hosts and mankind, enabling them to experience the divine presence in a mystical union.

Metropolitan Anthony of Sourozh

Also involved in the founding of the Monastery of Saint John the Baptist in Essex was arguably the most famous of the clerics who took up their ecclesiastical offices in Britain, Anthony (Blum, 1914-2003). Born in Lusanne, in Switzerland and a nephew on his maternal side of the eccentric composer Alexander Scriabin, he went on to become Metropolitan of Sourozh, the titular Russian Orthodox see of London. This had been established in 1962 and is now part of the Moscow Patriarchal Exarchate in Western Europe. Having originally qualified as a medical doctor in Paris, he became an eloquent and insightful spiritual conversationalist and preacher for the Russian diaspora in Britain and was a Russian Orthodox voice in the desert for the Moscow based Church, because of the freedom he enjoyed by being based in England and his broadcasting role on the BBC. Through such books as *Living Prayer* (1966), *Courage to Pray* (1973), and *The Living Body of Christ* (posthumously in 2007), he achieved a worldwide Orthodox following which grows year by year.

Unfortunately, in the years after his death, a schism broke out within the Russian Orthodox Church in Britain, between those who came from the old diaspora and were deeply influenced by Anglicanism and those who had recently arrived from post-Soviet Russia. Many initially separated themselves from the Russian Orthodox Church. However, this schism was eventually resolved by recourse to the High Court of England which decided in favor of the administrative authority of the Moscow Patriarchate. Most parishioners who had accepted the schism returned to the fold.

The Russian Orthodox Monastery of Saint Panteleimon, Mount Athos

While new monasteries and churches for the Russian Orthodox diaspora were being founded abroad, the ancient monastic seat of Russian Orthodoxy on Mount Athos, which had been founded as early as the eleventh century, suffered an almost terminal decline. Whereas in 1913 there had been some two thousand monks, by the 1960s there were only fourteen, a decline reflected in the other Orthodox monasteries of the autonomous state, now under Greek administration.[76] In 1968 a major fire also devastated its buildings. However, in recent years, the Monastery of Saint Panteleimon has undergone a major revival, both in terms of the strength of its brotherhood, as well as of its architectural fabric. Charles, Prince of Wales, has been one major global figure who has been a frequent visitor and contributed to its restoration. By 2016, there were some seventy monks, Ukrainian as well as Russian, serving in its ancient community.

Russian Monastery of Jerusalem

The Russian Orthodox Convent of Saint Mary Magdalene, on the Mount of Olives in Jerusalem, founded in 1847, also continued to function during these years of Diaspora. In 1936, a sisterhood was established here, attracting great fame for its holiness and devotion to pilgrims visiting the Holy Land. Later it became the earthly spiritual home of Prince Philip's mother, Princess Alice of Battenberg, who had become a nun. It also accommodates the relics of Grand Duchess Elisabeth, martyred by the Bolsheviks in 1918. Today it is under the authority of the Russian Orthodox Church Outside Russia. Nearby, just below the Mount of Olives, is a monastic community of monks, Saint Chariton, among others. Uniquely, the Gornensky Monastery is under the jurisdiction of the Patriarch of Moscow. With the immigration to Israel of many Soviet citizens, some of whom were Russian Orthodox, albeit many with at least some Jewish ancestry, the role of all of them within the wider Russian community has grown, as has their importance amongst a wider Orthodox context in a troubled region.

---

[76] Alfeev, *La Chiesa Ortodossa*, p. 322.

Chapter 10

The Church Revives

From the time of Mikhail Gorbachev's accession to power as General Secretary of the Communist Party of the Soviet Union in 1985, the position of the Russian Orthodox Church *vis-à-vis* the regime's authority began to improve, under the guidance of Patriarch Pimen (Izvekov). In 1988, Church and State joined together in the celebration of the Millennium of the Conversion of Rus by the Grand Prince Vladimir of Kiev.

The pace of change accelerated. While there were only some 7,000 Russian Orthodox parishes in the Soviet Union that same year, by 1989 their number grew to 11,000. This trend continued under Pimen's successor, Patriarch Alexei II (Ridiger, 1929-2008), who ascended the patriarchal throne in 1990. Thereafter, the Russian Orthodox Church enjoyed an even more extraordinary revival. By 2006, there were no fewer than 27,000 Russian Orthodox parishes in the territory of the former Soviet Union, and the number of monasteries had increased thirty-five times, to 713. Of these, 208 accommodated monks and 235 nuns in Russia; 89 monks and 84 nuns in Ukraine; and a further 38 monks and 54 nuns in the rest of the former Soviet territory. Beyond former Soviet borders there were two other monasteries for men and three convents for women. Together they served a Russian Orthodox population of over 160,000,000 adherents, making it by far the most populous Orthodox Church in the world. Obviously, the Russian Orthodox Church developed a vast infrastructure to supports its mission, in the social as well as religious sphere. This includes a wide spectrum of media: television, radio, films and, of course, the internet. There are also now five theological academies, to train clerics, one each in Moscow and St. Petersburg, in Russia, as well as in Kiev, Minsk, and Moldova. Additionally, there are two Orthodox universities, two institutes of theology, 37 seminaries, and 38 Orthodox high schools.[77]

Architectural and Artistic Revival of the Church's Fabric

A vast array of architectural and artistic revival was also carried out in the post-Soviet period. The most prominent church in Russia to be reconstructed was the Cathedral of Christ the Savior, in Moscow, rebuilt from the ground up in 1995-2000. The original edifice, which had taken forty-six years to build, and which had been the venue for the world premiere of Tchaikovsky's 1812 Overture, celebrating the defeat of Napoleon in Russia, had been blown up on Stalin's orders in 1931. He had intended for a vast Soviet palace, surmounted by a statue of Lenin, to be built in its stead. This failed, and the site became the site of the Moscow Swimming Pool. Then, in the post-Soviet period, it was decided to rebuild the cathedral, albeit in a slightly altered form. The architect Aleksei Denisov was at first commissioned to carry out the work, but it was completed by the artist and director of the Russian Academy of Art Zurab Tsereteli, who introduced modern elements into the design. These include the innovative use of bronze, rather than the original marble reliefs. Funds were provided by over a million contributors and work was carried out from 1992 to 2000. To the right of the cathedral are sculptures of Tsars Alexander II and Nicholas II.

Councils of Bishops in 2000 and 2004

In the new post-Soviet space, an important ecclesiastical priority was to hold a new Local Council which would not only clarify the administration and role of the Russian Orthodox Church in the new world of the Russian Federation and its predominantly Orthodox neighbors, but would remember what had befallen the Church during the Soviet period. The most important council of bishops held in Moscow since the Great Council of 1917-1918 took place in 2000. Its principal task was the canonization of thousands of martyrs and confessors who had died during the revolutionary era and Soviet decades of persecution. It also considered the relation of church, state, and the wider world. Significantly, it also provided the framework for relations with the hierarchy and adherents of other religious faiths. Moreover,

---

[77] Ibid., pp. 310–313.

within Orthodoxy, it had been ahead of its time in glorifying the Holy Royal Martyrs, the Holy New Martyrs, Saint John of Kronstadt and Saint Xenia of Petersburg, well before the fall of the Soviet state. Furthermore, whereas the catacomb Metropolitan Joseph was included on the list of New Martyrs by the ROCOR, the later Moscow glorification did not do so.

Four years later, a new council focused upon a wide range of issues, including improving relations between the Patriarchate of Moscow and the Church Abroad. This was just one effort, among others, to reestablish communion, and it continues to this day. Reconciliation was supported by Russia's temporal as well as ecclesiastical authorities. In 2006, a joint Act of Canonical Communion was passed by both Churches. In 2007, Patriarch Alexei II and Metropolitan Lavr of the Church Abroad signed the accord for each church respectively, allowing the latter considerable autonomy, albeit formally subordinated to that of Moscow. Metropolitan Lavr died in Jordanville, New York in 2008, but was succeeded by Metropolitan Hilarion Kapral and cooperation and intercommunion continues.

Restitution of Church Property

Many Orthodox churches have been restored by the Patriarchate of Moscow. However, ownership itself remained vested in the state, as remains the case with Roman Catholic houses of worship in France today. The Church came to depend on funding from government sources, rich sponsors, and the wider laity. In 2010, however, new laws sought to return houses of worship and ancillary buildings to the church. This has been an on-going process, which has awakened hostility from the secular world and from religious sects and non-believers. With the fall of the Iron Curtain, it became possible for outside religious groups to gain permission to preach in the former Soviet Union. From 1990 to 1997, Russia was among the freest places on earth in terms of legal protections for religious freedom. During that period, along with Baptists and Mormons, no less than five hundred newly arrived religious sects had begun to function, of which the Jehovah's Witness Church and Church of Scientology attracted many adherents. Both soon came to be perceived as threats not only to the Orthodox Church but also to the social fabric of Russian society. In 1997, a law was passed which curtailed missionary activity, in favor of supporting the "traditional" confessions of Russia, Russian Orthodoxy, Islam, Judaism, and Buddhism.

The Hierarchy of the Church Today

Administratively, the Russian Orthodox Church today is one of fifteen "local" Orthodox churches, that is, churches organized according to ethnic or historically defined communities of adherents. Composed of some 262 dioceses, 155 of which are in the Russian Federation, its head is the Patriarch of Moscow, who administers the Church together with the Most Holy Synod.

Historically candidates to the diaconate and priesthood had to reach the age of twenty-five. Today this has been lowered to eighteen, while bishops retire at 75, with the patriarch occupying his throne for life.

Most priests are married parish clergymen, otherwise known as white clergy, rather than celibate monks, or black clergy, who form a small minority of the clerical order. Candidates for the priesthood are not permitted to marry after their ordination, however, nor if they become widowers or are divorced. If they do, they are generally obliged to return to the laity.

In today's largely secular world, it may surprise many to know that the Russian Orthodox Church benefits from an abundance of young people with a spiritual vocation, a situation unknown since imperial days and unrivalled in the churches of Western Europe. As of 2013, there were some 27,000 Russian Orthodox priests serving a faithful flock of 160 million people, out of a total world-wide of some 227 million.[78]

The Patriarch of Moscow and all Rus, the autocephalous primate of the Russian Orthodox Church, was a position first assumed in 1589. As such, he is its chief administrator, in conjunction with fellow bishops and the Most Holy Synod. As such, he does not rule over the Russian Orthodox Church, as the pope does over the Roman Catholic Church. While he has canonical authority over the diocese of Moscow, the other metropolitans, archbishops, and bishops retain theirs over their own.

A bishop administers in conjunction with his fellow bishops. This confirms the concept of *sobornost*, which is central to Orthodoxy. Bishops

---

[78] Alfeev, *La Chiesa Ortodossa*, p. 341, p. 357.

only have jurisdiction in their territories, though excommunications are valid everywhere. Supreme dogmatic authority rests in the council, which includes bishops, other clerics, and members of the laity. The government of the Church rests with the council of bishops and presbyters, who are representatives of their bishops and can only celebrate the liturgy with the latter's authorization. Between the sittings of these councils, the Patriarch, together with the Holy Synod, governs the church.

Below them in the hierarchy of ecclesiastics are archimandrites, that is, monk-priests who serve as abbots over monasteries or otherwise exercise prominent authority roles in the Church. The lower clergy is composed of secular priests who may marry before their consecration, but not afterwards, and priest-monks who generally live within monastic communities. Monks take vows of poverty, chastity, and obedience and mainly live in monasteries based on the Rule of Saint Basil the Great, a monk of the fourth century AD. There are no differing orders, as in Roman Catholicism or Anglicanism, following the disciplines of different saints. Priests are often assisted by deacons in their liturgical practice. Women are not permitted to be priests, following Biblical injunction which reserves Holy Orders exclusively for men. Many become nuns and some abbesses, running convents for other nuns. These nuns serve the Church in a plethora of ways.

Metropolitan Kallistos

Among leading contemporary Orthodox theologians, those of the greatest importance include, in the United Kingdom, Kallistos (Timothy Ware, 1934-), titular Metropolitan of Dioclea, in modern-day Turkey. Raised in the Anglican Communion, he converted to Orthodoxy as a young man and was Spalding Lecturer for Eastern Orthodox Studies at Oxford from 1966 to 2001. He is also on the Board of Directors of the Orthodox Institute at Cambridge. Among his numerous works are *The Orthodox Church* (1963), *The Orthodox Way* (1979), and *Orthodox Theology in the 21st Century* (2012). In 2017, the Archbishop of Canterbury awarded him the Lambeth Cross for Ecumenism, "for his outstanding contribution to dialogue between the Anglican and Orthodox Churches," and he is a popular figure in Russian Orthodox circles, clerical as well as lay.

Metropolitan John

John (Zizioulas, 1931-), titular Greek Orthodox Metropolitan of Pergamon since 1986, is another spiritual leader who has had immense influence on Russian Orthodox theologians. He trained under Georges Florovsky and thus was educated in the tradition of the Russian Orthodox Church. He later became Professor of Patristics at the University of Edinburgh before moving to the University of Glasgow as Professor of Systematic Theology. His works study the important role of bishops and the centrality of the Eucharist in congregational worship. Unusually for an Orthodox theologian, he draws upon the writings of the French existentialist author Albert Camus to support his views of man's ontological freedom as provided by the Holy Trinity, which frees man from his biological constraints and brings him to everlasting life. Among his noted works is *Communion & Otherness: Further Studies in Personhood and the Church* (2007).

Jean-Claude Larchet

Another great contemporary Orthodox theologian, who also derived influence from France, is Dr. Jean-Claude Larchet (1949-). Originally a Roman Catholic, he converted to Orthodoxy under the influence of the writings of Vladimir Lossky and Nikolai Berdyaev, whose spiritual father Serge Chevitch received him into the Church in 1971. He has written numerous works on patristics theology and among his most noted works are *Mental Disorders and Spiritual Healing* (2005) and *Theology of the Body* (2017).

Father John Behr

An Englishman, Father John Behr (1966-) is also of considerable significance because of the role he plays in the study of patristics in contemporary Orthodoxy. First studying under Ware, he initially focused on sexuality and asceticism in the second century church. A secular priest and former Dean of Saint Vladimir's Seminary, in Yonkers, New York, he became Professor of Patristics there focusing on Saint Irenaeus of Lyon. His major early works include *The Way to Nicaea* (2001), *The Nicene Faith* (2004), and *They Mystery of Christ. Life in Death* (2006). His more recent works include *Origen. First Principles* (2018) and *The Paschal Gospel: A Prologue to Theology* (2019).

Patriarch Kirill

Patriarch Kirill (Gundyaev, 1946-) is the primate of the Russian Orthodox Church, under whose auspices all Orthodox liturgies in Russia are held. He comes from a family deeply grounded in faith. His grandfather had been a prisoner of the gulag at Solovetsky Monastery, in the White Sea, and his father was a priest. Kirill trained at the Leningrad Theological Academy, where his older brother was a professor. Although he is a keen supporter of President Putin and a strong Russian state, he is also very open to collaboration with the hierarchies of other religious faiths, including the mainstream Protestant churches and, in particular, the Roman Catholic Church. His meeting with Pope Francis, in Havana in 2016, was the first time a patriarch and pope had met in person. They went on to sign a declaration of thirty points, which addressed a variety of issues, on some of which they agreed and on others they agreed to deal with in the future, in the hope that eventually a full unity of Christians could be achieved without compromising sacred truths. Today, the Russian Orthodox and Roman Catholic Churches share common stances on the value of family life, a horror of abortion and the reserve of the priesthood for men. However, with respect to non-traditional religious sects, such as the Seventh Day Adventist Church, Mennonites, and the Church of Scientology, the Patriarch is not a supporter of toleration, fearing that they undermine the mainstream religious values of traditional Christianity. Moreover, with respect to the Ecumenical Patriarch, he has broken all relations, even to the degree of imposing a prohibition on the receiving of sacraments in churches under the latter's authority. This has occurred not for reasons of dogma or spiritual disagreements but because of the latter's unilateral decree of autonomy to the breakaway Orthodox Church in Ukraine. The Patriarch's notable spiritual writings include *Freedom and Responsibility: A Search for Harmony-Human Rights and Personal Dignity* (2011), in which the treasures of an Orthodox and traditionalist value system are contrasted with those of a liberal, secular and individualist one.

Metropolitan Hilarion (Alfeev)

Hilarion (Alfeev, 1966-), titular Metropolitan of Volokolamsk, has a very important role in the hierarchy of the Russian Orthodox Church as chairman of the Department of External Church Relations and is one of the Patriarch's most important assistants. He is also a permanent member of the Holy Synod. On the one hand he has been a keen proponent of ecumenism, while on the other he has been unflinching in refusing to compromise on core tenets of faith and spiritual values. A highly cultured and deeply spiritual church leader, he studied at the Tchaikovsky Conservatory, in Moscow, before attending the Moscow Theological Academy and Oxford, where he studied under Ware. He is deeply rooted in the Western classical tradition of music, especially that of Johann Sebastian Bach, and has composed many religious musical works, including his own *Saint Matthew's Passion* (2007), *Christmas Oratorio* (2008), and *Stabat Mater* (2012). He is also a prolific writer of books on Orthodoxy and has written the definitive work on that subject, *The Russian Orthodox Church*, which has appeared in Russian and other languages.

Metropolitan Tikhon (Shevkunov)

Another figure of great significance in the Russian Orthodox Church today is Tikhon (Shevkunov, 1958-), Metropolitan of Pskov and Porkhov. In contrast to Metropolitan Hilarion, Tikhon vociferously rejects any need for ecumenicism, preferring an uncompromising approach to other religions and to deviations from Orthodoxy. For him, all spiritual "Truth" is contained within Orthodoxy and therefore any ecumenical outreach would only compromise its values. Said to be the confessor of President Vladimir Putin, he has famously declared on a plethora of global media outlets that he is "no Cardinal Richelieu!"

Tikhon's faith seems to be of the most traditional kind, and he especially warns against dabbling with the spiritually esoteric, in particular, with mystical seances. In *Everyday Saints and Other Stories* by Tikhon, a Best Russian Book of the Year in 2012, he cites an experience in which an evil spirit posed as the author Nikolai Gogol to encourage Tikhon and the fellow students participating in such a seance to commit suicide. They resisted and vowed never again to engage with spirits in such a way. He also stresses the role of the elder in the Church *vis-à-vis* his flock. For example, he cites the example of a woman who, rather than follow the advice of the famed elder Archimandrite John (Krestiankin), at the Pskov Monastery of the Caves, not to undertake the medical operation recommended by her doctor, ignored the spiritual father's advice and died. Tikhon also nevertheless stresses the internal freedom of the individual to make his own choices. Moreover, he rejects any cult of personality or expressions of authoritarianism in his own ministry.

Metropolitan Tikhon has also been a great memorializer of the martyrs of the Soviet regime and took the initiative in and oversaw the foundation of a new house of worship, the Church of the Resurrection of Christ and the New Martyrs, at the Sretensky Monastery, in Lubyanka Street. It is situated near the old KGB headquarters (now FSB). It was originally founded in 1397 but had been closed in 1925. Proceeds from his aforementioned book were donated to the new reconstruction. Sometimes considered an arch-nationalist, he nonetheless lauds the spirituality of Archimandrite Serafim, the treasurer and elder of the Pskov Monastery of the Caves, who was born a German East Prussian baron. More controversial is the initiative he leads to examine whether or not the martyred imperial family were murdered as part of a ritual killing, by order of the Bolshevik Yakov Yurovsky, at Ekaterinburg, in July 1918. Some in the Church have objected to this investigation, seeing it as a revival of the anti-Semitism which in imperial days plagued some sections of the clergy and laity. Others, however, have seen it as an appropriate procedure to explore what exactly took place during the imperial family's martyrdom.

President Vladimir Putin

President Vladimir Putin has been perceived by many to be an adherent and powerful protector of the Russian Orthodox Church. This has meant that, following in the footsteps of his predecessor Boris Yeltsin, he has assisted the Church in restoring it finances to thrive and serve the country as in imperial times. In consequence of this and other measures, the Church has also recovered much of its property. This has enabled it to resume its spiritual and charitable role among the peoples of Russia, much as the Roman Catholic Church does in many countries of the world. Its status is not formally established, as is, for example, the Anglican Church, in the United

Kingdom, but some in both Russia and West are hostile to it for this and other reasons. British Professor Nicholas O'Shaughnessy, of Queen Mary College, University of London, has lumped Russian Orthodoxy with paganism and Christianity, in general, under the heading "Celestial Pseudo-Mysticism," writing with disdain:

> The Nazis preserved the form of religion and politicised it into a civic religion, while rejecting its existential content. Putin's Russia has not needed to do this, the Orthodox Church, rejected and then rehabilitated by Stalin, has always been a devout ancillary of the Russian leadership. God, therefore, is on the side of Russia: and he is moreover the Christian God rather than the abstract providence or pagan ersatz Valhalla evoked by the Nazis. This servicing of the existential needs of a dictatorship must be regarded as one of the great achievements of the pseudo-democracy.[79]

However, all that said, some have accused the Russian Orthodox Church of falling pray to a new Babylonian Captivity, a state of affairs in which the hierarchy of the Church is felt to be too closely aligned to the Kremlin. Now, with the war going on in Ukraine in the spring of 2022, this collaboration has proved to be especially controversial. Yet the reality is, the Russian Orthodox Church has not always been "a devout ancillary." On the contrary, its priests, monks, nuns, and laity have often been persecuted and even martyred by those ruling over them in Russian history. Moreover, cannot a connection between a Church and head of state also be said to a fact of Christianity in Britain and America as well? Her Majesty the Queen is regularly portrayed attending church wherever she is and the ancient English battlecry, from Shakespeare's play *Henry V*, "Cry God for Harry, England, and Saint George," has been evoked in both war and peace for British monarchs ever since. So, too, in the United States, where God is invariably invoked by almost all Republican politicians and some Democrats, even if no specific church is established.

---

[79] Nicholas O'Shaughnessy "Putin, Xi, and Hitler - Propaganda and the Paternity of Pseudo Democracy," *Defence Strategic Communications*. 2: Spring 2017, p. 121.

The Patriarchal Military Cathedral of the Resurrection

Certainly it is true today that the Russian Orthodox Church stands in as harmonious with the state's authorities of power, as it has ever had, especially with the military. Today the newest great house of worship to be built in Russia is the Patriarchal Military Cathedral of the Resurrection of Christ, in Patriot Park near Moscow. The Cathedral has been established to serve the needs of the military and to provide a powerful spiritual and architectural symbol bringing together the Russians as a people, their Church, and the Russian Armed Forces.

Dedicated to the 75th anniversary victory of the Soviet Union over Nazi Germany, it was consecrated in June 2020. Built in a nineteenth-century Russian Revivalist style, it looks back to ancient Rus but is constructed with the most modern technology and looks to great historical events for its principal inspiration. The achievements of the Red Army are depicted in the lustrous stained glass mosaics of the vault of the cathedral and, not without some controversy, images of Putin and even Stalin were to appear on the walls, not as a saintly figure but as the Soviet leader who exhorted his subjects to defend the Motherland with all their might. However, at the former's request depictions of neither individuals ultimately were included. The structure is informed by mathematical symbolism: to give just one example, one of the domes is 14.18 meters high, evocative of the 1,418 days during which the Second World War was fought. Its crowning feature is an icon of the Savior-Not-Made-by-Hands, beneath the central dome, which is the largest such mosaic image ever made. With the Cathedral of Hagia Sophia in Istanbul now returned to its Ottoman usage as a mosque, Moscow sees itself even more justified in calling itself the Third Rome and the most formidable bulwark of Orthodox Christianity. Yet this very status is fraught with its own dangers and the answer to the riddle of how to 'Render unto Caesar the things that are Caesar's, and unto God the things that are God's, (Matthew 22:21) have yet to be satisfactorily resolved. Yet whatever the temporal problems of the Russian Orthodox have been, whether favored by the secular state or persecuted, it's spiritual riches have remained as always a source of perpetual succor at all times and for all.

Patriarchs of the Russian Orthodox Church

Saint Job	1589-1605
Saint Hermogenes	1606-1612
Philaret	1619-1633
Joasaph I	1634-1640
Joseph	1642-1652
Nikon	1652-1666
Joasaph II	1667-1672
Pitirim	1672-1673
Ioakim	1674-1690
Adrian	1690-1700
Saint Tikhon	1917-1925
Sergei	1943-1944
Alexei I	1945-1970
Pimen	1971-1990
Alexei II	1990-2008
Kirill	2009-

Index

Lightning Source UK Ltd.
Milton Keynes UK
UKHW021830230123
415835UK00009B/627

9 781680 539066